FIELD GUIDE TO

NATIVE PLANTS
OF AUSTRALIA

A BAY BOOKS PUBLICATION
An imprint of HarperCollinsPublishers

Previously published in Australia in 1991 by Bay Books
Reprinted in 1992

Bay Books, of
CollinsAngus&Robertson Publishers Pty Limited
A division of HarperCollinsPublishers (Australia) Pty Limited
25 Ryde Road, Pymble NSW 2073, Australia

HarperCollinsPublishers (New Zealand) Limited
31 View Road, Glenfield, Auckland 10, New Zealand

HarperCollinsPublishers Limited
77– 85 Fulham Palace Road, London W6 8JB, United Kingdom

National Library of Australia
Card number and ISBN 0 85835 904 9

Printed in Singapore

5 4 3 2
95 94 93 92

FIELD GUIDE TO

NATIVE PLANTS OF AUSTRALIA

Compiled by the editors and writers of
The Living Australia magazine

BayBooks
An imprint of HarperCollins*Publishers*

Contents

Plant
Communities

Where did the Australian flora come from? How did it get here? And why is it so different from that of the rest of the world? The remarkable adaptations of these plants, their tenacity and resilience, bear witness to a constant struggle of survival. Here we seek to explain how plants, like the rest of the natural world, are bound together by their environment.

The plants of the Australian bush have a homogeneity which is quite unique to the continent. This is a direct result of continental drift. 180 million years ago when the single landmass of Pangea split into two, Laurasia constituted the northern continents and Gondwanaland consisted of Australasia, Antarctica, India, Africa and South America. India and Africa drifted away approximately 65 million years ago leaving Antarctica sandwiched between Australasia and South America.

Today many similarities, both of flora and fauna, remain between these two continents as a result of migration via Antarctica. In the plant kingdom perhaps the most obvious example is that of the Protaceae family, 44 genera of which live in South or Central America and 95 in Australasia.

When the three continents began splitting up about 40 million years ago Australia drifted into a less temperate zone. The warmer, drier climate put enormous pressure on the plant community. Many became extinct while others adopted special characteristics to cope with their new environment, forming a distinctive Australian flora.

Some of the original plant forms continued to survive in the damper coastal areas. Others gradually evolved in the infertile soils of much of the continent to form today's sclerophyll vegetation. These are members of the well-known Protaceae, Myrtaceae, Epacridaceae and Fabaceae families. Still others, such as the saltbush (Chenopodiaceae family), the widespread acacias (Mimosaceae), the emu bushes (Myoporaceae) and daisies (Asteraceae) diversified in other ways to colonise the drier areas of the interior.

When the Australian and South East Asian plates collided 15 million years ago it promoted an exchange of seeds between the landmasses. The Antarctic beech, inherited from the time when Antarctica was still attached to Australia, spread into Asia, and tropical flora such as ginger, bananas, pitcher plants and white cedars migrated to Australia.

Within a single genus certain species have continued to diversify, making new adaptations and colonising new habitats. Some species of the eucalypts, grevilleas and banksias, though generally suited to poor soils, now occupy a place in the tropical forests of Queensland and the Northern Territory, while some boronias and lilies, usually preferring moist conditions, have come to live in the arid zones of the continent. This process of evolution continues unseen,with its inevitable extinctions and its constant adjustments of lifeforms,to fill every ecological niche the continent of Australia has to offer.

Brett Gregory

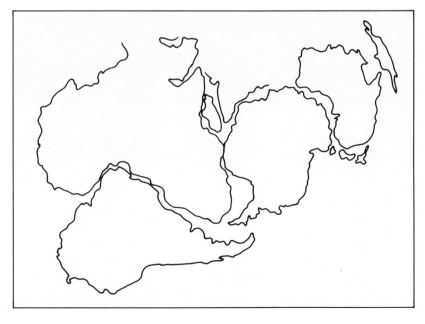

Antarctic beech (top right) growing in the temperate rainforests of Barrington Tops. Gondwanaland (right) during the Jurassic period, before the continents broke up.

Bay Picture Library

Arid and semi-arid regions

These areas are characterised by red rock, dried-up river beds, low scrub and hummocks of porcupine grass (*Triodia irritans*). Rainfall is irregular and unreliable and in central Australia it may be less than 250 mm a year. Summer temperatures are ferocious and on winter nights it can drop to −7°C.

The most dominant perennial of central Australia is the hardy mulga bush (*Acacia aneura*), whose silvery leaves are designed to reflect the intense sunlight and reduce heat absorption. The same silvery grey leaves are found on the ubiquitous saltbush (*Atriplex* spp.), whose vast expanses stretch across the flatness of the Nullarbor Plain.

The *Eremophila* genus, sometimes known as poverty bush because of its ability to survive even the mulgas in times of drought, displays other leaf adaptations adopted by plants in hot dry regions, to ward off the effects of dessicating winds and to prevent water loss. Some species are covered in fine hairs to maintain an insulating layer of air close to the leaf surface, while the leaves of others are coated with a sticky or varnish-like covering.

The parakeelya (*Calandrinia balonesis*), which is sometimes an annual and sometimes a biennial, has developed fleshy leaves and stems in which it stores water. Found around the saltlakes of the interior, this storage device is able to maintain clumps of pretty pinkish mauve flowers approximately four centimetres in diameter.

These dried up regions may seem inhospitable and unable to support much colourful vegetation, but appearances can be deceptive and lying dormant in the apparently barren soil are the tough-coated seeds of hundreds of thousands of short-lived annuals called 'ephemerals'. When the rains come the seeds take root and the stark landscape transforms into a soft living carpet of colour.

Perhaps the most stunning of these annuals is the military red and black flowers of the low-creeping Sturt's desert pea (*Clianthus formosus*), but for sheer density of blooms the mauves and yellows of the papery daisy petals are hard to beat. Yet within eight weeks or so the flowers have completed their cycles and scattered the seeds of the next generation upon a once-more parched land. There, they will bide their time until the next downpour. And it can be a long wait.

Perennials, too, are able to survive harsh conditions provided they have adaptive mechanisms. In sheltered spots where moisture collects and is slow to evaporate, species of hakea and grevillea will sometimes grow. Here also may be found desert oaks (*Casuarina decaisneana*) and bloodwoods (*Eucalyptus terminalis*).

From rocky outcrops the shimmering white bark of ghost gums (*E. papuana*) can be seen against an unrelenting blue sky. Near creeks and beside run-offs from rock formations the red river gums (*E. camaldulensis*) and the white cypress pines (*Callitris columellaris*) take up residence. These plant communities have seized the chance to fill ecological niches, even in the

The silvery grey vegetation (top left) typical of arid inland regions. Daisy and hops (right) growing in the Flinders Ranges following a downpour of rain. The mallee is the name given to semi-arid areas where mallee gums (below) proliferate. The thin branches that spring, sometimes directly from the soil, are supported by underground lignotubers. This characteristic formation is an adaptation to a very dry climate.

Jean-Paul Ferrero Auscape Int

remotest and hottest places in Australia.

Heathland

This other type of open vegetation does not so much suffer from lack of rainfall as paucity of soil. Much of Australia's soil is sandy and lacking in nitrogen, potassium, and most particularly phosphate. Although heathlands do occur inland, such as in the sandstone areas of the Grampians in Victoria, they are most common along the southeast, east, and west coastal strips. Often heathland plants have to contend with wind, salinity, leeching and poor drainage. Despite these conditions an abundance of flowering plants are found here.

The typical Australian heath plants (Epacridaceae family) like their northern hemisphere counterparts, Ericaeae, are particularly tolerant of poor soils. Sprawling populations of the ubiquitous pea family (Papilionaceae), with their nitrogen-fixing nodules, are at home here and in the peaty hollows, lilies enjoy a sheltered and damp position. Species of feather flowers, orchids and guinea flowers frequent this habitat too.

Above this lower strata grow some of Australia's best loved and most characteristic bushes, nearly all of them members of the Proteaceae family. The hakeas, geebungs, banksias, grevilleas, waratahs and in Western Australia the dryandras have all colonised these infertile regions. In response to the environ-

ment these plants have developed tough, woody leaves, botanically referred to as sclerophyllous. The high carbon content of such leaves minimises the plants' nutrient requirements.

In addition to these, heathland scrub frequently contains acacias, eucalypts, tea-trees and casuarinas, and grasstrees (*Xanthorrhoea Australis*) are found dominating such landscapes. Many of these plants are well equipped to deal with the hazards of fire and have even turned it to their advantage.

The hard seed capsules of several heath plants actually require heat and desiccation to burst open their pods and disperse the seeds. If structural damage is caused by fire, combat devices have developed to ensure regeneration. Some have underground lignotubers able to store food for immediate growth. Others have dormant buds beneath a thick bark just waiting for the fire to stir them into activity. Still others produce green leaves directly onto the woody trunks and branches so that the plant will continue to manufacture food for its regrowth. These remarkable adaptations ensure the survival of heath communities.

The scarlet blooms of a waratah bush (below) bring a splash of colour to this coastal heathland landscape in the Royal National Park, near Sydney.

Brett Gregory

Woodlands (left) develop in open country where sunlight is plentiful but the yellow grass shown here testifies to a scarcity of water.

Jean-Paul Ferrero Auscape Int

On the Atherton Tableland an abundance of vegetation jostles for a place in the rainforest (above).

Woodlands and sclerophyll forests

The woodlands of Australia stretch in a discontinuous band from western Victoria, within the Great Divide, up to the northernmost tip of Queensland and across the Northern Territory as far as the Kimberleys. There are also pockets in the southwest of Western Australia. The dominant vegetation is sclerophyll evergreens, chiefly eucalypts and acacias.

Woodlands are generally more open habitats than the denser wet and dry sclerophyll forests. With more room to spare, the trees spread their branches over a wider area and are shorter than their forest-dwelling relatives where competition for light encourages tall straight growth with a high canopy of leaves. Woodlands border or merge with scrub and grassland where herbaceous plants, such as irises, orchids and lilies grow close to the ground.

The floral compositions vary according to the region. In southeast Queensland the brigalow takes its name from one specific species of wattle (*Acacia harpophylla*). In the north a monsoonal climate suits *Eucalyptus tetrodonta* and *E. miniata* best. More temperate climates invite associations of yellow-box (*E.*

melliodora), red gum (*E. blakelyi*), white box (*E. albens*) and peppermint gum (*E. odorata*), while in Western Australia the York gum (*E. foecunda*) and raspberry jam (*Acacia acuminata*) frequently form communities.

The forests are the result of a higher quotient of soil nutrients and rainfall and they occur all along the eastern seaboard, in much of Tasmania and in the southwest corner of Western Australia.

The dry sclerophyll forests cannot support the grandest trees but many grow to 100 feet on relatively infertile soil. There are usually two or more species of eucalypt living in association with one another — red stringybark (*E. macrorhyncha*) with scribbly gum (*E. rossii*) are a common combination. The canopy is more closed than in woodlands but sunlight can still reach the forest floor, allowing hard and succulent-leaved shrubs to take root.

Wet sclerophyll forests consist of stands of eucalypts up to 200 ft high and they occur wherever there is enough moisture to sustain such growth. The canopy creates a closed habitat resulting in little sunlight and therefore minimal understorey growth. Probably the finest representatives of this type are the karris (*E. diversicolor*) of Western Australia but the mountain ash (*E. regnans*) of more temperate regions and the blue gums (*E. saligna*), blackbutts (*E. pilularis*) and flooded gums (*E. grandis*) of New South Wales and Queensland also form impressive forests.

Jean-Paul Ferrero Auscape Int

Brett Gregory

In the infertile soils of dry sclerophyll forests (left) herbaceous plants and shrubs take a hold and trees grow to a medium height. In the wet sclerophyll forests (above) the trunks are usually tall and straight reaching up to the light and the understorey consists most commonly of tree ferns.

Where the canopy of the rainforest has caved in (below) the sunlit gap is quickly colonised by new plants.

Closed forests or rainforests

Ecologists divide this habitat into three types: temperate, subtropical and tropical. The temperate rainforests are mostly found at high altitudes in Tasmania and Victoria but pockets exist as far as the McPherson Ranges on the New South Wales/Queensland border. As the warm air from the coast is forced to rise, clouds collect on the mountain tops and fall as rain, which then sweeps down into the gullies and through the matted undergrowth of lichens, mosses, orchids and ferns. The lichens and ferns also creep along moist trunks and branches of trees.

A second storey is formed by native laurels, tree ferns and musk daisy bushes. The principal trees here are often Antarctic beeches (*Nothofagus moorei*) in the north or myrtle beeches (*N. cunninghamii*) in the south and southern sassafras (*Atherosperma moschatum*).

Lianas rarely occur in these regions but in the more northerly subtropical rainforests. Their clinging, hoisting tendrils wrap themselves around the trees as they make their way to the light. Here too the fern and orchid epiphytes tuck themselves into the hollows of a wider variety of trees.

Coachwoods (*Ceratopetalum apetalum*) and hoop pines (*Araucaria cunninghamii*) commonly dominate these forests, so do other members of the Araucaria family. You may also expect to see New South Wales sassafras (*Doryphora sassafras*), *Podocarpus* spp., possum wood (*Quintinia* spp.), *Sloanea* and *Cryptocarya*. Many subtropical trees are bearers of soft fruit enticing the birds and small mammals who unintentionally disperse the seeds, both from on high in the canopy of sun-seeking trees and in the rich leaf litter which supports a second, shade-tolerant strata of trees.

The most diverse plant communities in Australia however, occur in the wet tropical forests of the north, particularly on the eastern slopes of Queensland's coastal ranges. Here the vegetation is dense and varied. Vines, fungi, epiphytes, ferns, orchids, palms and hardwoods all vie for a piece of the action, and for most that means reaching for the sky. Here grow the tall lilly-pillies (*Acmena* spp.), black bean trees (*Castanospermum* spp.) rosewoods (*Dysoxylum*), fig trees (*Ficus* spp.), king palms (*Archontophoenix*) and the now rare red cedar (*Toona australis*).

Lawyer vines and strangler figs wrestle their way up the trees to the light while the mighty hardwoods spread a canopy of large, floppy leaves, designed to capture the sun's rays, enabling efficient photosynthesis for sturdy growth. In these ideal conditions of warmth and heavy rainfall, plants grow rapidly and life cycles are accelerated. Dead leaves on the forest floor are quickly broken down to provide nutrients for the next living organism.

We have all been slow to understand the delicate ecosystem of rainforests. Although the soil appears fertile because of its ability to maintain such a profusion of plant life, the nutritious topsoil is in fact very shallow, sometimes only a few inches deep. Left alone, the self-generating mechanisms work well and the balance is maintained but as soon as land is cleared the thin layer of topsoil is washed away. If the cleared land is maintained the damage is irreparable. If however, as has happened in the Daintree Forest, it is left, the plants will creep back to reclaim what is theirs.

Mangroves and other wetlands

Mangroves are the common name for certain shrubs and trees that grow in dense thickets along tidal estuaries, salt marshes and on muddy coasts. They occur in the tropics and subtropics and the majority of species belong to the Rhizophoraceae and Verbenaceae families.

There are some 29 species in Australia. They chiefly occur in Arnhem Land, the Gulf of Carpentaria, Western Australia and down the coast from Queensland to South Australia.

The mangroves are supported in the mud by their tangled roots which sometimes grow horizontally. These trees live in almost airless soil and the protruding roots, known as pneumatophores, become their respiratory organs.

Mangroves spread by offshoots from mature trees and also by seed. In most species, the young plant develops in the fruit while still attached to the tree and eventually falls with the taproot already developed.

The roots trap debris, seaweed and sand thereby raising the seabed and contributing to the reclamation of land. They stabilise the shoreline and provide a safe habitat for a wide variety of fish, birds, crustaceans, molluscs and other wildlife. The more scientists study mangroves, the more they are being valued for their ecological role.

Inland wetlands are not well developed in Australia due to low rainfall and the low relief of the land. They often occur only seasonally and trees such as the baobab (*Adansonia gregorii*) and bottle trees (*Brachychiton rupestre*),

The roots of mangrove trees (below) poke out of a muddy surface at low tide. These pneumatophores allow the plant to 'breathe'.

The isolated marshes (above) give shelter to a diversity of plant and animal life. They are increasingly under threat from drainage and irrigation schemes.

both natives of the monsoonal north, have evolved fat, bulbous trunks for the storage of water in times of drought.

The rivers of the northwest and the Gulf of Carpentaria flood regularly every summer covering extensive areas of flat arid soil with shallow freshwater, while in the southeast the Murray Darling river systems flood across the plains at unpredictable times. The more permanent marshes, such as Macquarie Marshes, maintain an ideal habitat for many species of birds and small animals. Its inaccessibility and the abundance of bullrushes, reeds, sedges and perennial grasses provide good nesting grounds and shelter while the water assures a plentiful supply of insect larvae.

60 per cent of Australia's marshes have been destroyed or interfered with to a serious extent. Only recently have they become recognized as a valuable and delicate ecosystem that can benefit people and wildlife alike. The ibis alone kills millions of grasshoppers every year. What more effective pesticide could there be than this?

Alpine and subalpine regions

These regions occur in Tasmania, Victoria, New South Wales and the Australian Capital Territory. They contain numerous species of small shrubs, grasses, ferns, and rushes: annuals and perennials equal in beauty and diversity to the alpine flora of the northern hemisphere.

Conditions for vegetation in the snow country are exacting. Plants are subjected to strong and gale force winds, snow cover in winter, heavy rainstorms in summer, a short growing season restricted by frosts and, over much of the area in summer, day-long exposure to the sun.

Within this country, plant habitats vary according to exposure to wind, depth and permanence of snow, moisture and soil type. They may be woody, semi-woody or herbaceous but most are under one metre in height.

Woody or semi-woody shrubs are either dwarf or prostrate in habit, often spreading over rock faces. The leaves are small to avoid being torn by the wind and they are protected by inrolled edges, leathery or hairy surfaces.

Herbaceous plants are mostly in tufts, rosettes or prostrate mats while a few, like the hard-cushioned plant, *Colobanthus pulvinatus*, make compact cushions.

As in other more favourable areas, the plants grow in communities which characterise the various sections of the alpine zone — the herbfields, heath, feldmark, fens and bogs.

Flourishing in large communities through the wettest sections of the tall alpine herbfields, are the sod tussock grasslands and the beautiful mountain gentian, *Gentianella diemensis*.

Areas of well-drained, stony soils, the heath, provide homes for various small shrubs including the hairy-podded golden shaggy pea, *Oxylobium ellipticum*, and the variable alpine grevillea, *Grevillea australis*, with its small clusters of heavily perfumed, creamy flowers.

In valleys and depressions, bogs and more acid fens, a most important member of the plant community is the big moss, *Sphagnum*. The yellow-green cushions of foliage absorb enormous amounts of water which, during the dry season, trickle steadily away in clear streams.

Most testing of all the alpine habitats is the feldmark or fjaeldmark, the stone fields. These occur on the coldest wind-exposed ridges where any protective covering of snow may be swept away in winter leaving the plants vulnerable to freezing and desiccating blasts.

It also includes the leeward slopes where snow drifts may lie from one year to the next. Yet here, sheltering in rock crevices, is found the lovely anemone buttercup, *Ranunculus anemoneus*. Here too, across the stony wind-swept stretches, grows the white-flowered coral heath, *Epacris microphylla*, and snow heath, *E. petrophila*. These prostrate shrubs creep slowly over the ground gaining perhaps 10 millimetres in twelve months.

At Mount Kosciusko during the brief summer months masses of small, ground-hugging plants (above) flower and complete their life cycles. Their dispersed seeds will lie dormant through the freezing winter conditions to await the next thaw.

In alpine regions stony outcrops (below) provide tussock grasses and cushion plants with shelter against wind, snow and frost. Their tufted structure provides them with a micro-climate for added protection.

Bush Natives

It is hard sometimes to remember that the lavish displays of fruits and flowers and the sweet perfumes of plants are not intended for our own gratification but rather they are designed to lure the many birds, bees, butterflies and small animals on whom they depend for their pollination and seed dispersal. If you want these plants in your garden you must try and make them feel at home: this section tells you where 'home' is for some of Australia's best-loved species.

GREVILLEAS

Large and diverse family

Bay Picture Library

One of Australia's most spectacular trees, the grevilleas belong to an unusual family of some 250 members: tall and short, red, yellow and green, many of them with characteristics so distinguished, they could be totally different plants.

All but about 20 of the species are peculiar to Australia, the exceptions having also reached New Caledonia and other Pacific Islands. Western Australia is the richest in these splendidly flowering trees which take their name from C. F. Greville, one of the founders of the Royal Agricultural Society.

Grevillea bipinnatifida (above) has prickly leaves and large pendulous, toothbrush-type flower spikes. It is often found as a sprawling plant and has been added to many rockery gardens. Occurs in Western Australia.

Making a brilliant golden-yellow spire in late winter or early spring is the silky oak, *Grevillea robusta*. When in flower, it is one of Australia's most spectacular trees. Although it has been cultivated in many places, its native habitat is along the creeks of the well-watered forests of the coastal areas of southern Queensland and northern New South Wales and inland as far as the Bunya Mountains. The silky oak is the tallest of the 250 known species of grevilleas.

Grevilleas range in size from prostrate ground-hugging plants like the dark red flowered *G. lauriflora* from the Blue Mountains and *G. confertifolia* from the Grampians to trees 20 to 30 metres in height, like the silky oak and the beefwood, *G. striata*. The creamy flower spikes of the beefwood brighten the dry inland reaches in spring, but most make shrubby bushes from one to five metres in height. Some species find homes in the mountains of Tasmania and the Southern Alps, in the arid areas of Central Australia and the flower-rich southwest corner of Western Australia as well as in the well-watered coastal lands of the east.

Turn over a new leaf

The leaves of the grevilleas are as diverse in size and shape as the plants and, when mature, may be light to dark green, grey or grey-green. The reverse side of the leaves is often covered with fine hairs, bronze, grey or silver. The young foliage is likely to be bright green, sometimes reddish. In texture the leaves may be soft or leathery, harsh or hairy, often prickly and sharply pointed. In shape they may be simple ovals or ellipses, long, narrow and pointed, needle-like or sharply lobed like a holly leaf. Although the individual flower shapes are varied, the differences are not as great as in the leaves. In all grevilleas the petals are fused into a small tube which may be straight or curled into a shell shape while some have a one-sided swelling at the base.

The flowerheads take various shapes: they may be cylindrical with the flowers arranged evenly around a central stem, 'tooth-brush' or comb-like with the flowers packed along one side of the stalk, in erect or pendulous clusters or in a loose, open head. Many grevilleas are called 'spider flower' because the long styles resemble spiders' legs.

All shades

Flower colours range through white and shades of cream, pink, red, yellow and orange, with occasional ones in green, grey, mauve or brown. Quite a number are perfumed including *G. biternata*, *G. leucopteris* and *G. brevicuspis* but not everyone enjoys the scent.

Flowering time depends not only on the species but where the plant is growing. Some seem

Bank's grevillea, *G. banksii* was one of the first to be used in gardens. Cylindrical flower spikes are usually red but may be cream. The flower spikes appear throughout the year and they occur in Queensland.

G. dielsiana grows to 1.5 metres high and among the prickly foliage grows these beautiful clusters of red or red-orange flowers. The flowers bloom in spring and early summer and are common in Western Australia.

The silky oak, *G. robusta*, is a tall erect tree loaded with golden flowers. Regarded as Australia's most spectacular tree it grows along creeks in the coastal areas of southern Queensland and northern New South Wales.

The leaves on the *G. obtusifolia* are smooth dull green but the flowers appear in vibrantly coloured clusters of green and red. Occurs in New South Wales in spring.

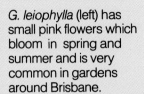

G. thelmanniana (far left) is a popular ground cover with red flowers. Sometimes occurs as a shrub and is found in Western Australia.

G. leiophylla (left) has small pink flowers which bloom in spring and summer and is very common in gardens around Brisbane.

Pink spider flower (far left), *G. sericea* is found in New South Wales only and its white to deep pink flowers appear throughout the year. Like most grevilleas needs a well-drained position.

The sprawling *G. biternata* (left) has a fine green foliage covered in spring with small white scented flowers. The prostrate form originated in Western Australia but has since spread east.

G. annulifera (far left) bears its flowers in cylindrical spikes which bloom in spring. Occurs in Western Australia and introduction to the east coast has not been successful.

This species, *G. wilsonii* (left) is possibly one of the showiest of them all. The red flowers appear in spring among the prickly leaves. Occurs in Western Australia with some successful plants in Canberra.

never to be without a few blooms but many produce their nectar-filled blossoms in winter and spring, providing food for many honey-eating birds such as the little friar birds, yellow throated miners and rainbow lorikeets. The lorikeets are particularly attracted to the 'tooth-brush' flowers of the silky oak which are so filled with nectar that shaking the branches can produce nectar rain.

Grevilleas have attracted much research interest and there are several major groups of cultivators on the market already. These cultivators are being grown overseas extensively especially in California and other warm areas of the United States, South Africa and New Zealand. Grevilleas have only just begun to be appreciated by Australians in home gardens, although local councils have been planting them as street trees and shrubs for many years. ●

TROPICAL AND SUBTROPICAL TREES

Life in the jungle

Esther Beaton Auscape International

Many tropical and subtropical trees, especially those bearing brilliant flowers, are seen in cultivation in climates and habitats far removed from their natural ones. They have been planted in our nineteenth-century public parks, used to line our streets and malls and bought from nurseries to decorate our private gardens. Their native habitats however are often some of the wildest places in Australia.

The golden spiky anthers of the silky oak, *Grevillea robusta*, are an invitation to the acrobatic crimson rosella, *Platycerus elegans*, of the Queensland rainforests.

The stunning red flowers and the strikingly-shaped leaves of the Queensland firewheel tree, *Stenocarpus sinuatus*, make this tree easy to recognise.

A large proportion of our native trees and shrubs fall into the tropical and sub-tropical categories. The richest source of this type of flora is in the rainforests of Australia. In the northern Queensland rainforests there are 1,000 tree species, a large component of which are distinctively Australian and many of which produce the most beautiful flowers.

Spectacular flowering trees

The Queensland firewheel tree, *Stenocarpus sinuatus*, which occurs up to the Daintree River in the north and as far south as the coastal rainforest of the Bellingen River, also grows in Papua New Guinea. As many as 12 to 20 scarlet flowers are produced from one point, like the spokes in a wheel, and together they span ten centimetres in diameter.

Another of the same genus, the white-flowering scrub beefwood, *Stenocarpus salignus*, occurs on the tablelands and in coastal rainforest from the Illawarra district in New South Wales, up along the coast of Queensland. Like the firewheel tree, it thrives in a medium to heavy well-drained soil.

The *Oreocallis,* also a member of the Proteaceae family, is a genus of seven species, only two of which are found in Australia. The *Oreocallis pinnata,* the southern waratah tree, is tall and majestic, with a long straight trunk and a large crown. It flowers in summer with bright orange-red paired flowers crowded into spectacular heads at the ends of the branches. It is found in the coastal rainforests from Dorrigo to beyond the Queensland border. The northern *Oreocallis wickhamii,* is similar to the southern waratah tree and occurs on the Atherton tablelands and north of the Daintree River. It is best suited to a heavy to medium moist soil.

Often the leaves in tropical and subtropical rainforests are fleshy and large. This is to absorb as much light in the twilight rainforest world as possible. The leaves often obscure the beauty of the flowers. The spring flowers of the black bean or Moreton Bay chestnut, *Castanospermum australe,* are not easily seen against the dense glossy foliage since they grow well down the branches on the old wood and along the main trunk. They are large yellow-green to orange-red pea flowers which grow in loose racemes or spikes. They appear in great profusion and are rich in nectar. This tree occurs in the New Hebrides, New Caledonia and in the northern coastal districts of New South Wales and Queensland.

Origins

Not all the trees that grow naturally in these regions are confined to Australia. Many are part of the Indomalayan type of flora, though they can be found in patches all the way down

The fruits born from the white-whorled flowers of the scrub beefwood, *Stenocarpus salignus*, may be up to ten centimetres long.

The scarlet blooms of the waratah tree, *Oreocallis wickhamii*, are not always easy to see as the crown often forms part of the rainforest canopy.

The black bean tree, *Castanospermum australe*, with its yellow and red pea-flowers and a four-centimetre bean pod, is a member of the Papilionaceae family.

The Moreton Bay fig, *Ficus macrophylla*, is a large, spreading tree suitable for open parklands but if planted out in most gardens it will eventually threaten the house foundations.

The fallen trunks of these myrtle beeches, *Nothofagus cunninghamii*, will decompose quickly on the rainforest floor to provide succeeding plants with a nutrient-rich soil.

The cones of the bunya pine, *Araucaria bidwillii*, are very large and have been known to knock a person out passing underneath.

With no green leaves yet on the Illawarra flame tree, *Brachychiton acerifolius*, the bell-like flowers produce a blaze of colour when seen from a distance.

the east coast of Australia. This group includes all our native palms, the bangalow and the livistona, the walking stick palm, and the lawyer vine from which wicker furniture and baskets are made.

The fig trees (*Ficus* spp.), which are found naturally in Australia, are related to the Indomalayan banyan tree. The Port Jackson fig, *Ficus rubiginosa* grows as far south as Bateman's Bay. Many figs, such as *Ficus microcarpa* var. *hillii*, grow as pot plants and as street trees in Sydney since they can withstand salt spray. Its natural habitat is the dense scrubs of Queensland, stretching all the way to South East Asia and China. The Moreton Bay fig, *Ficus macrophylla*, which is widespread in coastal scrub and on the Dividing Range of Queensland and northern New South Wales, however is confined to Australia.

Antarctic or niggerhead beech, *Nothofagus moorei*, and myrtle beech, *N. cunninghamii*, of the Fagaceae family, are related to beeches of the northern hemisphere, and are found in South America, New Zealand and New Guinea. Their presence on this continent contributes to the whole theory of continental drift. Remains of tropical rainforest trees such as beeches have been found in Antarctica. This evidence confirms the now widely-accepted belief that the southern continents were all once one landmass.

The Antarctic beech is found in northern New South Wales on the Barrington Tops and in the Macpherson Ranges. It is a marvellous straight tree, spectacular in groups, with thick rough bark and beautiful leaves which are arranged in fan-like sprays. The young foliage is orangy red. The myrtle beech occurs in the temperate rainforests of both Tasmania and Victoria but it is at home even in snow. It is a very ancient tree and, like the Antarctic beech, it is thought to have originated from Gondwanaland, which in the Jurassic period constituted the three southern continents.

The mighty pines

Also straying northwards to the tropics from their original birthplace in Antarctica, are members of the Araucaria genus. To the European eye these tall straight trees, with their curious stiff evergreen branches, were considered bizarre. They became popular as domestic trees and today they are commonly seen in old gardens and parks.

The Araucariaceae family has about 18 species, mainly found throughout the tropical and subtropical south west Pacific region and South America. Australia's two species are perhaps, besides the eucalypts, our best-known and-loved trees: the bunya pine, *Araucaria bidwillii*, named after the naturalist John Bidwill, who died while collecting plants in

The silky oak, with its soft pretty leaves and golden influorescences, has become a very popular tree in gardens along the east coast. It grows well in most soils and needs full sunlight to produce its best flowers.

The umbrella tree, *Schefflera actinophylla*, is a good container plant and grows well in gardens in warm areas.

the Queensland bush, and the hoop pine, *Araucaria cunninghamii*, named for Alan Cunningham, one of the first directors to the Sydney Botanic Gardens.

The bunya bunya is found in the southern Queensland rainforests and has a dome-shaped crown. Its cones, which contain edible seeds, are up to 30 centimetres long and 20 centimetres wide. Its leaves, yellowish green and delicate when young, turn a dark green with very sharp stiff tips when mature.

The hoop pine occurs from the rainforests of the Macpherson Ranges in northern New South Wales to the coastal scrubs of the far north of Queensland. The ends of its spreading branches are like feather dusters, with the flower cones crowded at the tips. The trunk is dark brown and marked by horizontal wrinkles. It is a common tree for roadside planting, parks and farms.

The Queensland kauri pine, *Agathis robusta*, is also among this group of Antarctic rainforest trees. In its natural habitat it is a majestic,

slow-growing giant of a tree which can reach 52 metres. It grows in the valley bottoms of rainforests, on flats and on the slopes of coastal ranges.

The Macpherson Overlap

Where the two types of flora, one from the southern continents and the other from the northern islands of South East Asia, mix in the forests of northern New South Wales and southern Queensland, you get an area known as The Macpherson Overlap. Here the mixture of planting from two hemispheres is unique in the world.

The highly-prized red cedar

Another magnificent tree is the red cedar, *Toona australis*. It is not related to the northern hemisphere cedars but is a hardwood of considerable value. It has a beautiful patina and is easy to work. In the past it was popular for furniture-making and interior design. As a result of indiscriminate logging it has become extremely rare in accessible areas though its boles are still being lifted out by helicopter in remoter regions.

Monsoonal trees

In the far north monsoonal species have evolved in the rhythms of the wet and dry seasons. They drop their leaves briefly at the end of the dry season, flower and then produce new foliage.

The jacaranda, so common here as to be almost naturalised but in fact a native of the Amazon in South America, is one of these. Also the Illawarra flame tree, *Brachychiton acerifolium*, the Queensland lace bark tree, *Brachychiton discolor*, and the silky oak, *Grevillea robusta*, are three tall monsoonal species which are among the few deciduous Australian plants.

The Daintree

The Daintree River is perhaps the richest area of tropical trees in Australia. Here a single hectare of rainforest may contain over 150 different tree species and many plants are still to be botanically described and named.

The umbrella tree, *Schefflera actinophylla*, is seen here. Its red-flowered curved spikes are a favourite with the hordes of noisy rainbow and scaly-breasted lorikeets.

Like the well-publicised fate of the Daintree, rainforests everywhere in Australia are under threat. The economic interest of tropical hardwoods and concern for jobs in the timber trade are being weighed against the conservationists' arguments for the maintaining of virgin rainforests. The outcome of this debate will determine the future of many of our finest trees.

FEATHER FLOWERS

Flowers of venus

ANT I.R. McCann

These are probably the most beautiful of all flowering shrubs, a contention indicated by their scientific name, Verticordia. The verticordias belong to the Myrtle family; the myrtle tree was sacred to Venus; and one of Venus's titles was Verticordia (from the Latin *vertere,* to turn; *cor*, the heart). To turn the heart was something which Venus did to all the men who saw her. Which all goes to show that botanists have a very convoluted way of thinking. The flower's common name which describes their feathery petals was conceived by simple men.

The painted feather flower is a common species on the Western Australian sandheaths.

The cauliflower bush, *V. brownii,* with *V. pritzelii* in the foreground. The cauliflower bush reaches about 60 centimetres in height, and is often seen along roadsides in Western Australia.

There are 40 to 50 known species of feather flowers. One, the tree feather flower, *V. cunninghamii,* spreads from the north-west coast to the Gulf country of Queensland; another, *V. wilhelmii,* grows on the Eyre Peninsula and Kangaroo Island, South Australia; and others are endemic to Western Australia.

Stay-at-homes

Feather flowers are seldom seen growing outside their native State, where they develop into shrubby plants, usually under 1 metre tall. The heath-like foliage and brilliantly coloured flowers are carried either in the upper leaf axils of the branches or in terminal clusters. They do not respond well to conditions outside their State. As they would beautify gardens anywhere, experimental work is being done to make them feel at home not only throughout Australia but in California, United States of America.

The feather flowers flourish on the sandplains and sandheaths where they grow into shrubby plants, usually under 1 metre tall. The heath-like foliage and brilliantly coloured flowers are carried either in the upper leaf axils of the branches or in terminal clusters.

Typical forms

Each flower has five calyx lobes which are coloured and conspicuously fringed or divided around the margin, and five rounded petals, which may be entire or fringed like the calyx. In some species there are petal-like, sterile stamens which are also finely divided. The colour range includes white, pinks, reds, yellows and mauves. Individual blooms are not more than 2.5 centimetres across but are often produced in such profusion that they may cover the entire bush.

The common cauliflower bush, *V. brownii,* with its even growth and rounded shape, 60 centimetres by 60 centimetres, is so closely covered with tiny, creamy-white flowers in late spring and early summer that it really does resemble a giant cauliflower. It grows on the verge of the roads or in other uncultivated areas of the wheatbelt — the cleared farming area of Western Australia — and further inland on the sandheaths. There is a pink-flowered form of *V. brownii* which grows close to the coast, east of Esperance.

Conspicuous petals

The painted feather flower, *V. picta,* is widespread in these sandy stretches. It grows from 0.5 – 1.0 metres tall with pairs of linear leaves, less than 1 centimetre long. Unlike most of the other species the unfringed, rounded, pink petals are much more conspicuous than the frill of

The flowers of the painted feather flower are only about 1 centimetre across, borne on a long stalk rising from a leaf axil.

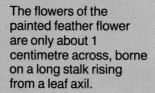

The yellow feather flower, *V. acerosa* bears its small rounded flowers in spring in moderately dense heads. The foliage of this species is variable on any one shrub, and may be rounded or long and narrow.

The brilliant red flowers of the scarlet feather flower make it the most spectacular of the feather flowers. It is not an easy plant to grow, but can be struck from cuttings and will grow and flower in pots.

The yellow feather flower, *V. chrysantha*, is similar to *V. acerosa* in many respects, but has linear leaves. It is one of the hardiest feather flowers under cultivation.

Claw feather flowers are heath-like plants, reaching a height of under 1 metre. The flowers are golden yellow at first, gradually changing to brownish-red.

The pink woolly feather flower, *V. monodelpha*, is a bushy shrub reaching about 1 metre. The pink flowers of this Western Australian appear in spring.

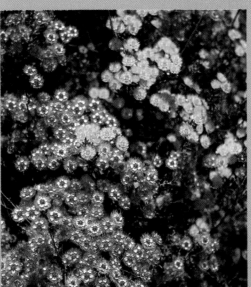

V. insignis, intermingled with *V. chrysantha* (the latter bearing yellow flowers). Feather flowers often appear in groups, adding to the brilliance of the display.

finely cut, pink calyx lobes below them. The flowers are small, only 1 centimetre across, each one on a long stalk rising from a leaf axil.

Further south on the sandheaths from Esperance to the north of Albany is the home of another feather flower with predominant petals. In the hidden feather flower, *V. habrantha*, the white petals, smooth and circular, almost completely hide the short, feathery calyx lobes. The plant is smaller than the painted feather flower reaching only 50 centimetres, the thick, narrow leaves up to 4 centimetres long and individual flowers less than 1 centimetre across.

Flowers of the spring

Two typical, spring-flowering, brightly-coloured feather flowers are found in the coastal sandplains north of Perth. The scarlet feather flower, *V. grandis*, is among the largest-flowered species. The shrub's growth is open, 1 – 2 metres tall, and the rounded leaves, up to 1.5 centimetres across, are neatly set in pairs along the stems. In spring, thickly fringed, vividly red flowers with long projecting styles rise from the upper leaf axils to form brilliant spikes.

The claw feather flower, *V. grandiflora*, grows further afield and is widespread from the north coast south east to Ravensthorpe. It is smaller than the scarlet feather flower, under 1 metre tall, with heath-like foliage. The shining yellow blooms, massed into terminal clusters, are also smaller, 1.5 centimetres in diameter. As they age their colour changes to brownish-red. The anthers have unusual claw-like appendages which give this verticordia its common name.

Two other similar, but smaller, golden-flowered verticordias are the yellow feather flowers, *V. chrysantha*, and *V. acerosa*. The former blooms from October to December. Its anthers are free of the appendages found on the claw feather flower. The latter, which also flowers in spring, has a variable foliage which may be long and narrow or rounded.

Rugged habitat

The granite outcrops, the rock islands, which are scattered throughout the south-west corner of Western Australia, provide habitat for the feather flower, *V. plumosa*. A variable shrub, it is often a small rounded bush 50 – 60 centimetres across with grey-green heath-like foliage and soft pink flowers, the calyx coarsely divided into short segments. The flower clusters may be open or massed into globular heads.

Another spring-flowering native of the granitic hills east of Perth, the variegated feather flower, *V. hueglii*, has clusters of very heavily fringed flowers which are creamy white on

opening but turn to red as they age. The variegated feather flower is a low spreading, open shrub with very narrow leaves about 0.5 centimetres long.

V. plumosa is a small rounded shrub reaching about 50 centimetres. The foliage is generally grey-green, and about 6 millimetres in length. The flowers, one of the more attractive of the group, appear in spring.

Atypical flowering

Not all verticordias flower in the spring. On the south coast sandheaths around Esperance, *V. sieberi* produces its small pale pink flowers in late summer and autumn. This is also true of *V. minutiflora* whose thickly clustered pale pink or white heads of bloom are made up of the smallest of all verticordia flowers.

The Wongan feather flower, *V. staminosa*, another of those living on the granite outcrops, is one of the few winter flowering verticordias. It is a spreading open shrub whose branches are covered with short bristles. The leaves are needle-like and the feathery, yellow flowers, opening in August, have long projecting red stamens. The blooms are not massed in conspicuous clusters. The rapier feather flower, *V. mitchelliana*, a feather flower with a difference is another of the wheatbelt verticordias. It makes a shrub 0.5—1.0 metres tall by 1 metre wide and the grey-green foliage contrasts strongly with vivid red, pendulous, fluffy flowers which hang below the spreading branches. The prominent yellow styles, 3 centimetres long which sweep out from each bloom, give the plant its common name.

V. muelleriana is one of the tallest feather flowers, and bears flowers outside the normal colour range of feather flowers.

Atypical colouring

Some feather flowers have colouring outside the yellow-pink-red range. They include *V. muelleriana,* one of the tallest species, whose maroon flowers are produced through late spring and summer, and *V. oculata* whose leaves are rounded and whose 2 centimetre flowers are mauve and silvery-white.

The eastern feather flower, *V. wilhelmii*, is similar to the Western Australian species. It prefers sandy, well-drained soils and grows into a small shrub with heath-like foliage. The white flowers are in terminal clusters, the fringed calyx lobes larger than the smooth petals and the stamens tipped with red anthers.

The silvery-white edging of V. oculata's flowers show clearly how the group was named. The fine, lace-like border bears a striking resemblance to small feathers.

Tropical species

The feather flower of the tropical north, the tree verticordia, *V. cunninghamii*, is not a small shrub like its southern relatives but is quite large, sometimes even becoming a small tree 6 metres tall. The foliage is still needle-like, the leaves 1 – 1.5 centimetres long, and the creamy-white flowers clustered at the ends of the branches have rounded petals above feathery calyx ruffs, deep red anthers and projecting styles. Like its southern counterparts, it grows in sandy places or on well-drained sandstone hills. ●

A spreading plant with great cultivation prospects, the rapier feather flower bears bright red flowers in early summer. It is quickly gaining popularity in gardens, and will probably help to establish other species of feather flower.

BANKSIAS

A history lesson

Banksia belong to the family Proteaceae, from Proteus, the Greek god of the sea who could assume any shape he chose. Banksia are also named in honour of Sir Joseph Banks who spent a small fortune studying Australian flora and made his crew and his greyhounds suffer for prosperity.

The banksia genus is a distinctive group of about 60 species confined almost entirely to Australia; one known exception is *B. dentata* which is also found in New Guinea. Two species, *B. ericifolia* and *B. serrata*, were among the first specimens of native plants collected by Sir Joseph Banks in 1770, when he was among the first white men to land on the east coast of Australia.

Sir Joseph Banks

A.N.T. R & D Keller

Banksia coccinea or scarlet banksia (above) is possibly the most spectacular of all the banksias. Native to Western Australia but are successfully growing on limestone underlay in South Australia.

At this period in England there was great interest in all aspects of natural science and wealthy people were prepared to spend their money simply to further knowledge of such subjects. Joseph Banks shared this interest and had ample means and influential friends to help him pursue it.

When it was decided to send an expedition under Captain Cook to the southern hemisphere to observe the transit of the planet Venus, Banks obtained permission to sail on the *Endeavour* with Cook to collect and study the unknown flora and fauna they expected to find.

With him went his personal servants and greyhounds, and a party of nine assistants. Included in the group was a prominent Swedish naturalist, Dr Carl Solander, and Sydney Parkinson, a fine artist and botanical draughtsman whose skills, in the days before cameras, were essential to record their discoveries. A library of natural history books, great quantities of apparatus for collecting and preserving animal and plant specimens and containers for seeds were essential luggage. All this had to be stowed on a ship already carrying her crew and normal gear including livestock for food during the long voyage (there was no refrigeration): a ship less than three cricket pitches in length and not quite ten metres wide! The cost of Banks's party and the equipment was estimated by a contemporary at ten thousand pounds. The cost was borne by Banks himself: the discomforts were endured by everyone.

After twenty months at sea, calling at Madeira, Rio de Janeiro and Tahiti and circumnavigating New Zealand, the *Endeavour* anchored in Botany Bay. As the Aboriginals seemed hostile, the white visitors collected specimens along the foreshore for the first two days, but on 1 May 1770 they were able to go inland. As well as epacris, wattles and 'gum' trees — a name given to the eucalypts by Banks — specimens included the two banksias mentioned earlier, old man banksia (the saw banksia or red honeysuckle) and heath banksia.

All the specimens had to be drawn or painted before they wilted and died, and samples were pressed for herbarium collections. In his diary on 3 May Banks wrote: 'Our collection of plants was now grown so immensely large that it was necessary that some extraordinary care should be taken of them lest they should spoil in the books. I therefore this day . . . carried ashore all the drying papers, nearly 200 quires . . . spreading them upon a sail in the sun . . . often turning them . . . By this means they came aboard at night in very good condition'.

The large number of plants collected in the vicinity and the use of the beach as a drying area led to the name of Botany Bay.

Of sixty or so species of banksia now known, about ten are endemic in the eastern half of mainland Australia and Tasmania. The rest occur in Western Australia, mostly in the southwest corner of the state, many among the tall forests of jarrah and karri.

In their natural habitats banksias are very hardy, growing in poor coastal soil exposed to harsh sea winds, on sandy heathland, in the Ninety Mile Desert of South Australia, in the infertile sandstone soils of the Blue Mountains and

Heath banksia, *B. ericifolia* (right) is a rounded shrub growing to about five metres. The small straight leaves are bright green. Distribution: New South Wales and Queensland.

The orange-red cob of the heath banksia (right).

The unopened flower head of the heath banksia (right). A hybrid of the heath banksia and *B. spinulosa* has been created and one unusual form of the heath banksia has black leaves.

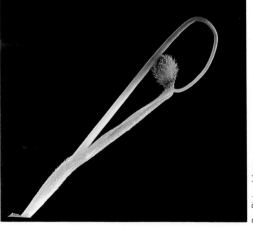

The single flower spike of the heath banksia (right). Even singly the flowers of the banksia are beautiful.

Bay Picture Library

A.N.T. R & D Keller

A.N.T.

Bay Picture Library

Saw banksia, *B. serrata* is a gnarled shrub that is given extra character by dried out old cones on the tree. The saw banksia (left) is very common along the coast and is resistant to salt spray. Common source of food for honeyeaters like small possums.

B. serratifolia, the wallum banksia (left), is very similar to the saw banksia but its leaves are more intensely toothed. Common in New South Wales and Queensland.

Hairpin banksia, *B. spinulosa* (left), has orange-yellow flowers which attract a plethora of birdlife. Some plants develop a much darker flower. Common in New South Wales, Queensland and Victoria.

The possum banksia, *B. baueri* (left), is so named because of the 'woolliness' of the flower head when it dies. In full bloom the flowers are still a brownish-grey.

the Grampians, and even in the Australian Alps. Although they favour sandy, well-drained places some have adapted to swamp areas. All the eastern species are frost hardy except *B. dentata*.

All banksias are evergreen, ranging from trees of 18 metres or more in height, generally with gnarled, contorted trunks and dark, deeply indented bark, through shrubby types to some which are prostrate. Of these some actually bury their branches and sometimes their leaves in the sandy soil, only the flowering heads appearing above the surface. Some banksias which grow in shallow soil low in nutrients have a highly specialised system of feeding roots forming a close network just below the surface. In this way they make use of any phosphate released by fires before it is leached through the soil.

Banksias also display a great range in the size and configuration of their stiff leaves and the size and colour of the flower spikes. The simple leaves, most of which have saw-toothed margins, may be from 7 to 30 centimetres or more in length, the upper surface smooth, often dark green and the underside frequently covered with grey, white or tawny felt. In some the young growth is entirely covered with fine hairs. Diverse leaf shapes include those which are long and thin, the heath-leafed banksia, *B. ericifolia*, and the hairpin banksia, *B. spinulosa*; those deeply cut into triangular segments such as the bull banksia, *B. grandis*, and the showy banksia, *B. speciosa*; and those with smooth or wavy margins with only an occasional sharp point, the holly-leafed banksia, *B. ilicifolia*, and the coast banksia or white honeysuckle, *B. integrifolia*.

The cylindrical flower spikes or 'cobs', from 5 to over 30 centimetres in length, glow among the dark foliage in vibrant shades of yellow, gold, orange and scarlet or a more muted greenish-yellow. The large cobs of the possum banksia, *B. baueri*, appear brownish-grey, the pale yellow flowers being hidden behind long, soft, woolly hairs.

A thousand tubular flowers

There may be as many as a thousand slender, tubular flowers spiralling around a woody central axis in each head. In each flower the long narrow structure called the style is trapped at the tip in the tube, forming an elongated loop. When the flower opens the style may straighten out or retain its hairpin shape, a feature which helps to identify the species.

Glowing flowers rich in nectar

Banksia flowers are rich in nectar and pollen, giving rise to the common name 'honeysuckle', although none actually resemble the twining plant traditionally given that name. The sweet nectar attracts bees and other insects and also honey-eating birds and tiny marsupials such as the pygmy and honey possums and the dibbler.

A.N.T. R & D Keller

Orange or acorn banksia, *B. prionotes* (left), has narrow toothed leaves and orange flower spikes which display in winter. This plant has flowered in the eastern States but its real home is Western Australia.

A.N.T. R & D Keller

B. ornata or desert banksia is a two metre shrub common in Victoria and South Australia. The flower heads appear in summer and autumn.

Bay Picture Library

This species of banksia (left) grows along the ground. It has triangular toothed leaves and a yellow flower cob. To date this species, *B. prostrata*, has been found only in Western Australia.

A.N.T. A H Burbridge

A honey bee (left) approaches to steal the pollen of the Menzies banksia, *B. menziesii*. The tree usually stands six or seven metres but a dwarf variety has been developed. The pink/red and silver flowers appear in autumn. Found in Western Australia.

Insect predators follow their prey among the flowers and all this trafficking around the flower spike transfers the pollen from one flower to another. Black cockatoos, the largest of the cockatoo family, have hooked beaks powerful enough to tear open the woody seed containers and release the seeds on which they feed. They also tear off branches as thick as a man's thumb, possibly in an attempt to get at the larvae of the wood-boring insects which they relish.

Aboriginal people sought the banksia flowers for their sweetness, some soaked the flowers in water to make a sweet drink called *beal*, others struck the heads against their hands and then licked off the nectar. If there were enough flowers the women collected the nectar in a *coolamon* (a shallow vessel) by hitting the flowers against the sides, sometimes gathering as much as half a litre, but they had to be up early before the honey-eating birds.

The gumnut babies

When the flowers die they remain on the central spike, forming a dry, grey-brown bristly fuzz. Those successfully pollinated develop into seed containers (botanically, follicles), each a pair of tightly closed, velvet-covered woody growths looking like swollen eyelids. In some species where only a few emerge they give the cob a strangely humanoid appearance — a fact which led authoress May Gibbs to use the cobs of old man banksia as models for the bad banksia men in her stories of the gumnut babies, Snugglepot and Cuddlepie.

Each follicle holds two seeds with fine papery wings which are released when the woody case is opened by the heat of a fire. Once free they germinate rapidly in ash and will probably reach flowering stage in three or four years. The exception is the coastal banksia or white honey-suckle, *B. integrifolia*, which does not wait for a bushfire but spits its seeds out precipitously once they are ripe. Gardeners wishing to obtain seed should put the dry head with its unopened seed containers on a tray in an oven at 120°C for an hour, or in a container such as a glass jar in a warm, dry spot until the follicles open, remembering to keep different species separate.

Most popular cultivated plants

Some banksia species are killed by bushfires, relying on their seed for regeneration, but others, even when badly burnt, will grow again from lignotubers, the storage organs which form swellings at the base of the trunk.

Banksias are amongst the most popular cultivated native plants: in suitable conditions they grow easily with a minimum of attention. Unfortunately, many of the eye-catching western species do not flourish in the eastern states, principally because they fall victim to the root rot fungus. ●

HAKEAS

Well-travelled Australian natives

All the hakeas are either beautiful or curious and some are useful as well. In the useful category are those fast-growing species which provide shade and shelter, such as *H. eriantha*. Australians travelling abroad are often surprised to come upon this Australian native in parks or streets in the United States, South Africa and the Middle East. In these foreign parts it is a popular shade tree and, as it does not grow to great heights, can be planted under electricity wires with safety.

Hakea suaveolens is a rounded shrub reaching about three metres. In South Africa it has been classed as a weed, such is the ease with which it will spread.

Jean-Paul Ferrero

There are about 140 known species of *Hakea*. All of them are endemic to Australia but a few, like the silky hakea, *H. sericea*, have become naturalised overseas. Although different species are found growing in various localities right across Australia, more than half of them are native to the south-western corner of Western Australia. They are mostly shrubby plants, some developing into small trees.

Variation in form

Proteus, the old man of the sea, had the gift of prophecy but he eluded those who sought to consult him by assuming different shapes. Hakeas belong to the family Proteaceae, which derives its name from that of the changeable seer. As might be expected of plants belonging to such a family, the hakeas vary widely in form.

They have alternate leaves which vary in shape from long and narrow through cylindrical or flat, oblong, circular or fan-shaped to broadly linear. They may be simple, deeply lobed or divided with smooth or toothed margins but most have definite parallel veins and a leathery texture.

The flowers are very similar to those of grevilleas with long narrow tubes composed of four segments, which split and roll back from the mouth when the flower opens. The protruding style may be straight or hooked. Colours include white, cream, yellow and many shades of pink or red.

Hakea seeds, which remain viable for many years, are contained in hard, woody cases botanically known as follicles. In most species the seeds are not released unless the branch dies or the bush is damaged by fire. In some cases, even when the seed case has been split open by the heat, the two, single-winged seeds are not immediately freed, to burn on the hot ashes, but remain for some time attached to the follicle.

Well-loved garden species

Many of the hakeas are popular garden plants. One of the best-known, often planted for its rapid growth, is the willow-leaf hakea, *H. salicifolia* (syn. *H. saligna*) which, in its native habitat, is usually found near permanent streams in scrub and open forest from south-east Queensland through eastern New South Wales. It makes a small tree up to 8 metres tall with narrow, flat, sombre green leaves, 5–12 centimetres long, but no more than 1.5 centimetres wide. The fragrant white flowers are carried in small clusters in the leaf axils throughout the spring. The rounded, nut-like fruits, about 2 centimetres long, have a short beak at the tip and are covered with rough, warty protuberances.

If the willow-leaf hakea merges into the background, the royal hakea, *H. victoria*, stands out like the Telecommunications Tower on Black

The willow-leaf hakea is a fast-growing plant, ideal for use as a screen or divider. In many areas it is suitable for planting beneath power lines, as it grows to no more than 8 metres.

The flowers of the silky hakea occur in two forms — white and pink, but only the white form is found in the wild. Most grow to 4 metres, but a form found near Canberra reaches only 1 metre.

One of the best known hakea species is the pin-cushion hakea, an attractive plant reaching about 6 metres. The brilliant red flowers appear in autumn and early winter. In cultivation this species is particularly hardy and maintains a compact appearance.

The royal hakea makes a wonderful feature plant — its boldly varieagated foliage can hardly be missed. The flowers of this medium shrub are quite insignificant, but the leaves, marked in reds, greens and yellows, certainly make up for this.

The cork tree, a common species of inland Australia, produces its yellow, nectar-filled flowers in winter. The cork of this tree, as suggested by its name, is deeply-cleft and resembles bark.

Another view of *H. laurina,* the pin-cushion hakea, highlighting the white styles that protrude from the flower heads.

H. obtusa, a close ally of the pin-cushion hakea, is a low spreading shrub growing to about 1 metre. It is found on coastal hills in south-west Western Australia.

The flowers of *H. cinerea* are characterised by long protruding yellow styles. The flower heads are yellow-orange, and tightly compacted at the end of the stems.

Mountain. Growing in the heathlands of the south coast of Western Australia from the Gairdner River to Ravensthorpe, the vertical stems, sometimes reaching 3 metres, are clothed in large, prickly, concave leaves which cup the clusters of cream or pink flowers. At first these leaves, botanically floral ones, are green, veined and heavily marked in cream but as they age the cream is transformed into orange and then red, each leaf remaining on the plant for up to five years. There are also plain green, juvenile leaves at the base of the stems. This is the only native Western Australian plant with naturally variegated foliage, and only in its normal, hot, dry environment does the foliage obtain its most flamboyant shades.

Other hakeas with unusual and attractively shaped, although not brightly coloured, foliage include *H. baxteri, H. conchifolia* (scallops), *H. culcullata.* All are from Western Australia. *H. baxteri* is an upright shrub, about 3 metres tall, with serrated, fan-shaped leaves 6 centimetres across. It is spring flowering, producing clusters of white blooms. *H. conchifolia* is a smaller shrub about 1 metre in width and height, whose rounded leaves, folded over to enclose the tufts of pink or white flowers, resemble mussel shells. Scallops, a very open, erect shrub about 2 metres tall, has wavy-edged, bowl-shaped leaves, 7 centimetres across, which clasp the stem and cup bunches of deep pink, occasionally cream, flowers.

The needle bushes

A number of hakea species are often referred to as needle bushes or needlewoods, as their leaves are very long, narrow and sharply pointed. One of these, the silky hakea, *H. sericea,* is a dense, very prickly shrub about 4 metres tall which is sometimes grown as a barrier hedge. It gains its common name from the silky hairs on the young wood. The leaves are cylindrical, up to 9 centimetres long, stiff and very sharply pointed. The pink or white flowers grow in small groups in the leaf axils towards the ends of the branches and appear in winter and early spring. The brown, woody fruits, 2–3 centimetres long, have upturned pointed tips. The silky hakea is an east coast species growing naturally and prolifically on the coast and ranges of Tasmania, Victoria and New South Wales.

Other needlebushes include the hooked needlewood, *H. vittata,* from the east mallee country of Victoria. This species is also found in dry regions of South Australia, New South Wales and Queensland. It is a small spreading shrub, 2–5 metres tall, with hooked points on the long cylindrical leaves. The hard reddish timber was used at one time for making tobacco pipes. A closely related, but smaller growing species, the silver needlewood, *H. leucoptera,* is found in

A Western Australian species, *H. bucculenta* flowers in winter, the tapered flower spikes appearing on the old wood rather than on young shoots as in many other species.

A corkwood hakea in Uluru National Park, with the Olgas in the background. This species is able to contend with the harsh conditions of the outback by storing water in its roots, a fact the Aboriginals were well aware of. They used it as a source of water in dry times, even carrying the roots with them over long treks.

the dry interior where it is also known as the waterbush. Its roots, like those of some species of casuarina, bloodwood and wattle, contain drinkable watery sap, used by Aboriginals and possibly explorers, as a substitute for pure water. Cut into lengths, the pieces were stood on end on a container to allow the liquid to drain out or, with the ends plugged with clay, were carried while hunting or food gathering. The cylindrical leaves of the silver needlewood are straight and the summer flowers white.

Another needle bush, *H. teretifolia*, is better known as the dagger hakea. Its name refers to the woody fruits which are like broad, short daggers, about 3 centimetres long, with two lateral projections at the base forming the handles. Many of the other hakeas have smooth or warty rounded fruits, 2–3 centimetres across, but the white flowers of the cricket ball hakea, *H. platysperma*, a medium sized shrub of the needlewood type, are followed by fruits which are as large and solid as cricket balls, while the hooked capsules of the small-fruit hakea, *H. microcarpa*, found in the eastern States and Tasmania, are no more than 12 millimetres long and 4–5 millimetres across.

Pincushions

While many of the hakeas have small clusters of white or yellow flowers spread along the stems, some have 'pincushion' flowerheads or crowded tapering, cylindrical spikes. The pincushion hakea, *H. laurina*, is a large shrub found in south-west Western Australia but is also widely cultivated, here and abroad. The broadly-linear bluish-green leaves, up to 15 centimetres long, carry conspicuous parallel veins. The red flowers, at their peak in winter, are packed into rounded balls, the long, creamy-white styles projecting like pins from a pincushion, the whole flowerhead being about 5 centimetres across. The sea-urchin hakea, *H. petiolaris*, also from Western Australia, is a more upright, slightly smaller shrub with similar flowers.

Although there are species with longer flower spikes, the grass-leaf hakea, *H. francisiana*, is one of the loveliest of this type. It is a small tree or large shrub about 5 metres tall which grows on the sandy plains of Western Australia and South Australia. The broadly-linear leaves with prominent parallel veins may be 26 centimetres long and the tapering upright spikes of red or pink flowers, 3–9 centimetres long, rise from the leaf axils in winter or spring.

The candle-spiked hakea, *H. ruscifolia*, another of Western Australia's range of outstanding flowering shrubs, is a much smaller, rather open shrub to 2 metres with small, sharply pointed, oval leaves. Large numbers of terminal spikes of white flowers are produced in spring and summer. Yet another Western Australian, red pokers, *H. bucculenta*, is so attractive that, despite the difficulties in its cultivation, it is in demand as a garden ornamental. It is a large, upright shrub reaching 7 metres. The leaves are long and very narrow and the red flowers, appearing in winter, are carried in 6–12 centimetre flame-like spikes.

Spectacular bark

Although usually admired for their flowers or foliage, the bark of some hakeas, such as *H. suaveolens*, is also attractive. Classed as a medium shrub, this hakea has smooth, rounded trunks covered with silvery bark which is almost as pale as birch bark. The spreading head of grey-green foliage is scattered, in autumn and winter, with balls of white, scented flowers. The leaves are cylindrical and divided. The seeds germinate so freely that the shrub, introduced into New Zealand and South Africa, is now considered a weed in those countries.

Quite a different bark covers the trunk of the cork tree, *H. suberea*. The heavy trunk of this small, 6 metre tree, common in inland Australia and across the north, is covered in thick, deeply-cleft bark. The needle-type leaves may be 40 centimetres long and the spikes of yellow, nectar filled flowers, are produced in winter. This is one of the hakeas whose seeds are released as soon as they are ripe.

BUTTERFLY-LIKE SHRUBS

Native plants of beauty and utility

The orange-red blooms of the coral-vine, interspersed here with wild sarsaparilla, form a striking massed display.

ANT A&S Tingay

The pea bushes bring the wildness of the bush and the strangeness of the desert into the garden. Some of them provide ground cover, and others are shrubs. Some are delicately perfumed and all are beautiful. Some are shy beauties, others flamboyant.

Sturt's desert pea, bush pea, parrot pea, poison pea — there are dozens of different native Australian plants which are commonly called pea bushes but they all have one thing in common — they belong to the pea family, Leguminosae. Just as daisies, whether large or small, woody or herbaceous, all have the distinctive flower form, so the pea flowers are characteristic of one section of the pea family. This section, or sub-family, of nearly 400 genera, is now usually given the status of a full family, Papilionaceae, meaning 'butterfly', the name referring to the structure of the flowers.

The five irregular petals of each flower are so arranged that the largest one, the standard, is held upright, sometimes reflexed, at the back and two lateral ones, wings, are carried on either side of the two lowest which are partly joined together to form the boat-shaped keel. The keel holds the stamens and pistil. Seeds of pea flowers are carried in pods. Many pea family plants are cultivated for their edible seeds — peas, beans and peanuts — for their value as pasture — lucerne and clovers — or for their ornamental and perfumed flowers — lupins, brooms and sweet peas. A number provide nectar for bees.

A flamboyant species

Some of the most flamboyant of Australian native flowers belong to this group. One of the best known is Sturt's desert pea, *Clianthus formosus* (syn *C. dampiera*). At home in the arid, sandy regions of southern Australia, Sturt's desert pea is an annual which germinates rapidly after rain, forming a carpet up to 2 metres across. Its soft, greyish-green foliage, covered with

ANT J Bronwlie

long, silky hairs, makes a good background for the brilliant, 8 centimetre long, scarlet and black blooms. Less showy colour variations are sometimes seen.

Ground-hugging or climbing species

Other spreading, or climbing plants which belong among the pea flowers include the coral-peas, *Kennedia*. The sixteen or so species of coral-peas are either recumbent or vigorous climbers, nine of these being endemic to Western Australia. Most have large, bright red flowers with reflexed standards.

Running postman, *K. prostrata*, grows in all States. The leaves, used at one time for making tea, are composed of three, rounded leaflets with wavy margins and the rosy-red flowers, about 2 centimetres long, are touched with yellow at the base of the petals. The seeds, contained in flat pods, are long lived, germinating after years if given the right conditions.

Western Australia is home to the showy coral-vine, *K. coccinea*, whose bright, orange-red blooms are small but thickly massed in terminal clusters, and to the unusual black coral-pea, *K. nigricans*, which has long, narrow flowers of purplish-black with yellow centres.

Another well-known ground cover or twiner, *Hardenbergia violacea*, is also occasionally called coral-pea but is more often known as false sasparilla. It is widespread in the tablelands and coastal regions of all the eastern States and South Australia and is also cultivated. The leaves vary from broadly ovate to narrow lance-shaped but are always distinctly veined. Although most plants bear sprays of tiny purple blooms, mauve, white or pink forms are sometimes seen.

Eggs in the bush

Several groups of pea bushes also go by the endearingly absurd name of 'eggs-and-bacon' as the flowers in most species are yellow to orange often combined with brown or red. The name is most commonly applied to bitter-pea, *Daviesia*, parrot-pea, *Dillwynia*, bush-pea, *Pultanaea*, and *Eutaxia* which are mostly shrubs or small trees, endemic to and widespread in Australia.

Most of the 70 species of bitter-pea are confined to Western Australia but the hop bitter-pea, *Daviesia latifolia*, occurs in all the eastern States. It is an open upright or straggly shrub sometimes reaching 3 metres with tough, heavily-veined, dull green, ovate leaves to 8 centimetres long. In spring it bears thickly packed trusses of small yellow and brown flowers in the axils of the leaves. The seeds are in small, pointed, triangular pods. The foliage, as in many of the bitter-peas, contains a bitter substance and was used at one time as a substitute for hops. An exception to the more common yellow

ANT O Rogge

ANT R & D Keller

ANT G. Cheers

After good rains in sandy regions of interior South Australia, Sturt's desert pea (left) bursts into flower, forming a dense carpet several metres across.

The showy parrot-pea (right), *D. sericea*, is found in open forests in all States except Western Australia.

The large leaves of the running postman (left) were at one time used for making tea. This attractive species is found in all States.

The rosy bush-pea (right) is a rare shrub found only in the Grampians in Victoria, and here only on the highest peaks. Reaching about 1 metre in height, it is a difficult plant to cultivate.

Often called false sarsaparilla, *H. violacea* (left) produces deep violet flowers. Mauve, white and pink forms may also be seen.

The flowers of the broad wedge-pea (right) are the largest of its genus, reaching about 3 centimetres across, with the plant itself growing to 1 metre.

One of the bitter-peas (left) widespread in dry, rocky areas is the narrow-leaf bitter-pea, *D. virgata*. This species occurs in New South Wales, Victoria and South Australia.

Eutaxia microphylla (right) is the only member of its genus not restricted to Western Australia. It occurs in two forms — prostrate ground-hugging shrub, and a small branching shrub reaching over 1 metre in height.

flowered forms, the leafless bitter-pea, *D. brevifolia*, is common in dry heathland from Victoria across to Western Australia. It is a virtually leafless shrub, about 1 metre tall, with stiff, bluish-green, spine-tipped branchlets scattered in spring with small wine-red or apricot-coloured blooms.

Harbingers of spring

The parrot-peas, a smaller genus of about 20–25 species, are heath-like shrubs usually less than 1.75 metres tall. The needle-like leaves are channelled on the upper surface and the small flowers are crowded together in terminal clusters or along the stems.

The twisted parrot-pea, *Dillwynnia retorta*, (syn *D. ericifolia*), is very common on the east coast, particularly near Sydney and in the Blue Mountains. The narrow leaves have a distinctive twist. A mass of deep yellow and red-blotched little flowers cover the shrub in later winter and spring. There are usually two seeds in each swollen pod.

At home anywhere

The bush-peas, *Pultenaea*, with over 100 species, form the largest genus of pea flowers in Australia. They range from prostrate forms to shrubs the size of small trees, thriving in many ecologically varied situations, inhabiting montane areas, forests, heathland, peaty bogs and the arid inland. The yellow or yellow and red flowers are small but in some species are clustered into dense heads.

The large-leaf bush-pea, *P. daphnoides*, flourishes in sheltered gullies from Queensland south to Victoria and South Australia. It is also found in New Zealand. It makes a tall, upright shrub with 1–3 centimetre long, dark green leaves, broadest at the tip, whose mid-ribs project into points. The yellow flowers, large for the genus, are tinged with brown and clustered at the ends of the many short branchlets. The small pods, each holding two seeds, are only slightly inflated.

Eutaxia is a small genus of only eight known species which, with one exception, are all Western Australians. The odd-man-out, *E. microphylla*, is common in southern Australia where two forms grow, one low and prostrate, the other a branching shrub to 1 metre tall. In spring both forms are covered with little yellow and red flowers.

Dancing with joy

'Dancing with joy' is the meaning of the word 'Chorizema'. All but one of the eighteen or so species of the flame-peas, *Chorizema*, are endemic to Western Australia, but they are widely known because of the popularity of the heart-leaf flame-pea, *C. cordatum*, as a garden plant. Its orange, cerise and yellow flowers make a striking colour combination. The eastern flame-pea, *C. parviflorum*, a small sprawling shrub, is a native of Queensland and New South Wales. The leaves are no more than 2.5 centimetres long and the tiny brown and yellow flowers are held in loose spikes.

The flowers of the wedge-peas, *Gompholobium*, while still mostly yellow and red, are larger than those of the 'eggs-and-bacon' peas. Of all the species the broad wedge-pea, *G. latifolium*, has the largest flowers. They are about 3 centimetres across. The broad wedge-pea is an upright shrub, about 1 metre tall, the leaves are divided into 3 leaflets, and the pale yellow flowers at the base of the leaves appear from mid winter to spring. There are about 25 species endemic to Australia, over half of which are found in Western Australia. The wedge-peas gain their common mainland name from the wedge shape of the mature flower bud but in Tasmania they are called bladder peas because of their inflated seed pods.

Beautiful but deadly

The 40 or so different species of the poison pea, *Gastrolobium*, are confined almost entirely to Western Australia. They are attractive shrubs with showy flowers in the yellow to reddish-purple range of colours. Unfortunately the foliage of many species is poisonous to stock, particularly when the plants are in bloom. *G. grandiflorum*, known as wallflower poison, yilgarn or desert poison-bush, is found across Western Australia, Northern Territory and Queensland on stoney hills or in waterless sandy river beds. It makes a large shrub, 2 metres tall, with stiff, elliptical, dark green leaves carried in pairs, terminal sprays of red and purple flowers which are 10 centimetres long. The egg-shaped pods are covered by long, soft hairs. It is one of the poisonous species. Other attractive but poisonous peas, including both annual and perennial herbs, belong to the genus *Swainsona*, which has about 60 known species in Australia and one in New Zealand. The flowers may be purple, red or blue, occasionally yellow or white, and the tip of the broad keel is twisted or curves inwards. The Broughton or purple pea, *S. procumbens*, is generally a sprawling perennial but sometimes produces upright stems. The leaves, up to 18 centimetres long, have about 20 small, widely spaced, hairy leaflets and each spray of flowers may carry as many as twelve blue or rosy purple blooms, 2–3 centimetres wide with spirally twisted keels. The pods, 2–3 centimetres long, are inflated with deeply depressed sutures. Broughton peas tend to grow in damp clay soils in the warmer parts of the continent. Although the foliage is toxic it only affects stock if they graze heavily on it. They then refuse other feed and will eventually die. ●

GUINEA FLOWERS

Golden beauties of the West

The snake or climbing guinea flower is one of the few guinea flowers that responds to cultivation, thriving in all but frost prone areas.

ANT I.R McCann

There is not only safety in numbers: there is spectacle. A guinea flower seen in isolation is inconspicuous almost to the point of invisibility. Masses of them, on the other hand, are a sight to fill the heart with pleasure and to set it dancing. These flowers merit a less fiscal common name, a name which would suggest even a small measure of their golden loveliness. All that glisters is not gold.

The sunny yellow blooms of the guinea flower *Hibbertia*, so called because of their likeness to the golden coins, brighten the hearthlands, sand dunes, mountains and forests of temperate Australia. While a few species grow in New Guinea, Madagascar and New Caledonia, the majority, over 100 different species, are native to Australia and two-thirds of these are indigenous to Western Australia. They are mostly shrubby plants under one metre tall, but some are taller or make prostrate ground covers or twining climbers. The guinea flowers are evergreen with undivided leaves but these vary in shape from the short, narrow leaves of the bundled guinea flower, *Hibbertia fasciculata*, to the smooth elliptical leaves, up to 9 centimetres long, of the twining guinea flower, *H. dentata*. A few have toothed margins. The circular blooms, usually yellow, may be flat or cup-shaped with five petals, often notched or lobed. The arrangement and placing of the central cluster of stamens is important in their botanical classification.

Congenial immigrants

The guinea flowers were named after an English plant collector, George Hibbert, and were introduced to Europe in the late 18th century when specimens of the snake or climbing guinea flower, *H. scandens* (syn. *H. volubilis*) were grown in greenhouses. This is one of the most vigorous and easily grown of the guinea flowers, most of which do not respond to cultivation, being difficult to propagate and very susceptible to root rot.

The native habitat of *H. scandens* includes the coastal sands as well as moister, more sheltered areas of Queensland and New South Wales, where its stems trail across the dunes or twine up through other shrubs. The glossy green, stalkless leaves are covered with silky hairs on the underside. The flat bright yellow flowers, eight

The twining guinea flower is a slender climber that bears bright yellow flowers through spring and summer. It may be propagated from cuttings, and will look its best when trailed through other shrubs.

Bay Picture Library

The bundled guinea flower is widespread over heathlands from Queensland to South Australia, including Tasmania. The beautiful yellow flowers make a stunning sight, such as here at Wilson's Promontory, Victoria.

ANT G. Cheers

The climbing guinea flower is a fast growing species well suited to cultivation. Propagation is by seed or cutting. A light pruning will thicken the plant and enhance its value as a flowering ground cover.

Bay Picture Library

The erect guinea flower is a variable shrub, usually attaining a rounded shape about 60 centimetres tall. It is quite adaptable in cultivation, and will tolerate most aspects, provided a reasonable amount of light and drainage are given.

Auscape

The leaves, stems and calyces of the silky guinea flower are covered by fine, soft hairs from which it takes its name. It is a coastal species, favouring sand dunes and other well drained locations.

The centralian guinea flower, *H. glaberrima* (right), is found only in central Australia. A small, spreading shrub to 50 centimetres, it can often be seen on rocky hillsides.

H. miniata (below) is one of the rarest of the guinea flowers. A native of Western Australia, it has perhaps the most striking flowers of the group. It appears in nurseries only intermittently, and is not ideally suited to cultivation.

to nine centimetres across, have a scent which some people find almond-like, others unpleasant. The flowers which appear throughout the year are followed by clusters of shiny, bright red fruits the size of small peas.

The stalked guinea flower, *H. pedunculata*, is another of the few species which can generally be cultivated. An inhabitant of the open forests and coastal areas of New South Wales and Queensland, it is usually a low, spreading, twiggy shrub, not more than 20 centimetres high, with occasional short upright stems. Flowering occurs in late spring and summer when a mass of delicate, cup-shaped blooms, just over one centimetre across, open, their long stalks holding them above the fine, glossy, dark green foliage. A few flowers may occur intermittently through the rest of the year.

Eastern species

The twining guinea flower, *H. dentata*, is found on the coast from Queensland south to east Victoria. It prefers less sandy soils and moister conditions than the snake guinea flower, *H. scandens*. The oval green leaves, sometimes assuming a bronze or reddish tint, are smaller, five or six centimetres long, with small, widely spaced teeth on the margins. The four centimetre flowers, opening in spring, have narrower petals but their fruit is similar to that of the snake vine guinea flower.

Common but not commonplace

One of the most common of the Victorian *Hibbertias*, the erect guinea flower, *H. stricta*, is also found in Tasmania and in temperate areas of most other mainland states. Its habit varies with its environment but it usually forms a small, twiggy shrub, about 60 centimetres high. The foliage is fine, downy and dull grey-green. In spring the upright stems are thick with small, flat, yellow, almost stalkless blooms, one to two centimetres across with rounded petals which are lobed and heart-shaped. The few stamens, no more than nine, are clustered to one side.

Another widespread species, the silky guinea flower, *H. sericea*, is found mostly on sand dunes or other coastal habitats. It is a small shrub, 30–60 centimetres tall, and gains its name from the fine silky hairs which cover the stems, leaves and calyces. The narrow, grey-green leaves, less than 2.5 centimetres long, are huddled together behind the yellow, 2.5 centimetre flowers. In this species the petals are notched and the 10–16 stamens are grouped on one side of the pistil.

Adaptable types

The trailing guinea flower, *H. astrotricha* (syn *H. billardieri*), now more correctly known as *H. empetrifolia*, and the rough guinea flower, *H. aspera*, are both variable plants, suiting their growth to their environment. The trailing guinea flower may be a sprawling, open shrub, less than 15 centimetres high, on exposed and windswept sand dunes or grow to 1.2 metres in moist and sheltered woodland. It is found in the coastal regions of the eastern States. The straggling, often reddish stems, are long and wiry and the sparse foliage consists of tiny leaves lightly sprinkled on both sides with minute bristles. In spring, the bright yellow flowers are borne in such profusion that, although small, about six millimetres across, they completely hide the foliage.

The range of the rough guinea flower extends from central Queensland south to South Australia and includes Tasmania. The plant may be shrubby or, given different conditions, the trailing stems, seldom red, may clamber over other shrubs to a height of two metres or more. The rough-surfaced elliptical leaves, one to two centimetres long, and the scattered flowers are larger than those of the trailing guinea flower but the plants are somewhat similar.

Offshore relation

The stalkless, golden-yellow flowers of the spreading guinea flower, *H. procumbens*, another common Tasmanian member of this group, are larger still, being 2.5–3.5 centimetres across. True to the habit indicated by its common name, the prostrate, leafy stems of the species form a spreading mat, up to one metre or more across, occasionally becoming more upright.

The dull green leaves are variable in shape, both narrow and wide leafed forms being known. It flowers abundantly through spring and summer. The spreading guinea flower is not confined to Tasmania, where it is at home from sea level to mountain plateau, but is also seen in Victorian coastal stretches.

The tall poppies

Taller growing guinea flowers include the willow guinea flower, *H. salicifolia*, and the tall guinea flower, *H. saligna*. The former is a leafy shrub 3 metres tall. The narrow, willow-like leaves, varying in length from 2.5–10 centimetres, are in small clusters along the erect stems. The stalkless flowers are very small, usually about 0.5 centimetres across. Its range extends along coastal New South Wales into Queensland.

H. saligna, with its grey-green foliage, may reach two metres in height. The base of each narrow, lance-shaped leaf clasps the stem. The yellow flowers, about two centimetres in diameter, are scattered along the branches. The species thrives in damp and sheltered areas of eastern New South Wales.

Stay-at-home types

One of the most striking of the guinea flowers, *H. miniata*, grows naturally only in Western

ANT G. Cheers

Australia and, unfortunately, like so many Western Australian plants, is difficult to cultivate. It has rather soft foliage and large apricot-orange yellow flowers with dark purple anthers. Another Western Australian, *H. stellaris*, is a small rounded and sometimes prostrate shrub about 30 centimetres tall. The bright green foliage and reddish stems are covered with orange-yellow blooms several times a year. Other Western Australian guinea flowers include the shrubby *H. acerosa* with fine, needle-like leaves and paler yellow flowers with heart-shaped petals, as well as the mat-forming *H. montana*, whose large lemon-yellow blooms appear in late spring.

Not all guinea flowers are confined to coastal areas. Travellers in central Australia are likely to see *H. glabberrima* growing on the stony slopes. It makes a small spreading shrub, about 30–50 centimetres tall, with smooth leaves up to ten centimetres long but less than one centimetre wide. The yellow flowers are the typical five-petalled guinea flower, two to three centimetres across, with broad petals and a central boss of stamens. ●

The spreading guinea flower is a prostrate shrub, forming a mat about one metre across. It is a common species in Tasmania, but is also found in coastal Victoria. The attractive flowers, not borne above the plant on stems, may be seen through spring and summer.

LILIES OF THE FIELD

A *splash of colour*

ANT. G. Cheers

Lilies are both diverse and spectacular, and can be found in almost any habitat. There is great variety to be seen: some, like the Gymea lily, are quite tall, with large flowers that can not be missed on a bush walk; others are decidedly more subtle, but are still readily observed. The common thread that brings the lilies together is the unique beauty of their flowers.

Although there are no true lilies, *Lilium*, of Australian origin there are many other indigenous species of the lily family, *Liliaceae*, and a few, commonly known as lilies, belonging to closely related families. This latter group, which for the most part belongs to *Amaryllidaceae*, usually have larger and more resplendent flowers. The most conspicuous of them all are the giant or spear lilies, *Ooryanthes*.

The giant, or to give it its native name, Gymea lily, *Doryanthes excelsa*, is found in wooded coastal areas from Jervis Bay, New South Wales, north into Queensland. In spring and summer the stiff flower stems, up to 4 metres in height, emerge from the dense clumps of pale green, pointed, sword-like leaves, 2 metres long and 10 centimetres wide. A globular head of deep red bracts and red tubular flowers with long, narrow, spreading segments, is held at the tip of the flower stalk. The flower tubes are filled with nectar. Woody capsules follow the flowers and, when ripe, split to release the flat seeds.

Less well-known and not as spectacular, the spear lily, *D. palmeri*, also called the North Coast giant lily or the white-throated Gymea lily, is found in or near rocky, rainforest sites in northern New South Wales and Queensland. The leaves are fleshier and the flower stalk arches

The Gymea lily *Doryanthes excelsa*, is unmistakable, rising like a sentinel through the scrub. The stem may be 4 metres in height, carrying aloft the round head of deep red bracts. When not flowering, the plant looks very much like a clump of sword grass.

ANT I. R. McCann

The full beauty of the Gymea lily is only revealed by close examination — which is often difficult considering the height of the flowers. The flower tubes, filled with nectar, are often visited by honeyeaters and other nectar–loving birds.

ANT I. R. McCann

The trumpet–shaped flowers of the Darling lily, *Crinum flaccidum*, are sweetly scented. It is found throughout the flood plains of the Murray–Darling river system, where it was used by early settlers as a substitute for arrowroot.

The common fringe lily, *Thysanotus tuberosus* (far left) is one of the more spectacular lilies. The beautiful purple flowers, about 2.5 centimetres across, are only short lived, but are replaced throughout spring and summer.

ANT G. & R. Wilson

over, carrying the red-brown blooms along the underside. The flowers have pale throats and the segments are not as spreading.

The leaves of these giant lilies contain strong fibres which were used to make rope exhibited and awarded a prize at the Great Exhibition of 1851 in London. After roasting, the young flower stems and the roots were eaten by the Aboriginals.

Sweet-smelling trumpets

While not nearly as tall as the spear lilies, the Darling or Murray lily, *Crinum flaccidum*, has showy heads of 5–15 white, pale pink or rarely yellow, scented, trumpet-shaped flowers on thick, upright leafless stems up to 60 centimetres tall. The glossy, strap like leaves clustering about the base die down each year.

The Darling lily grows on the flood plains of the Murray–Darling river system, extending from western Queensland and New South Wales to Victoria and South Australia. In times of drought the thick contractile roots pull the bulb deep into the soil. The ovoid bulbs, 7–10 centimetres in diameter, were used by settlers to provide a substitute for arrowroot.

Another *Crinum*, the swamp lily, *C. pedunculatum*, is much taller with leaves up to 1 metre long and stems reaching 2 metres. It is found in damp, coastal areas of New South Wales and Queensland and is sometimes cultivated. The white flowers with their long, narrow segments and elongated stamens, have a spidery appearance.

Like the Darling lily, the garland lily, *Calostemma purpureum*, belongs to the Amaryllidaceae family and prefers damp conditions. The dark green fleshy, strap-like leaves, only about 30 centimetres in length and 1.5 centimetres wide, die down annually. The thick erect flower stem reaches about 50–60 centimetres in height and carries 8–20 stalked flowers in a loose, terminal cluster. The pink or deep red flowers, with a yellow spot at the base of the throat, are trumpet-shaped, the short tube dividing into 6 broad, rounded lobes.

Riverbank beauty

The garland lily grows along the banks of inland rivers in New South Wales, Victoria and South Australia. It is often cultivated for its attractive spring flowers. The fleshy, ovoid seeds frequently germinate before they are planted. A yellow flowered species, the yellow garland lily, *C. luteum*, is similar except for the colour of its blooms. Its habitat extends into Queensland. The foliage of the yellow garland lily is thought to be poisonous to stock.

While the loosely clustered white flowers of the Brisbane lily, *Eurycles cunninghami*, are similar in shape to those of the garland lily, the foliage is quite different. Each large bulb produces a few shovel-shaped, heavily veined leaves of glossy, dark green colour carried on long, upright stalks. These leaves normally die down each year.

The Brisbane lily is endemic to Australia and is found chiefly in Queensland and northern New South Wales. The similar, but larger, native Eucharist or Cardwell lily, *E. sylvestris*, ranges from northern New South Wales and Queensland into Malaysia. The upright flower stems may reach 50–60 centimetres in height.

Two of the smaller flowered members of the lily family, the flax lilies, *Dianella* spp. and the blue lilies, *Stypandra* spp. have loose, open heads of numerous starry blue flowers. The flax lilies are widespread, occurring across Australia and beyond. All species have tussocks of long, narrow leaves whose strong fibres make them suitable for basket work. Those of *D. revoluta* may be 40 centimetres long with inward-rolled edges. The branching flower stems of this species are usually about 1 metre tall and each flower has 6 bright blue segments and large yellow anthers.

Like the flowers, the globular blue fruits which follow are conspicuous in the open grasslands which this lily inhabits. The pale flax lily, *D. laevis*, is similar, with flat, narrow leaves and pale blue blooms. A Tasmanian species, *D. tasmanica*, is common in that island and extends into Victoria in shaded positions. The leaf margins have minute teeth and the deep blue berries, seen in late summer, are 1–2 centimetres long. There is still some confusion over the classification of these plants.

Grass-like leaves

Like the flax lilies, the six species of blue lily grow in a wide range of habitats. The tufted blue lily, *Stypandra caespitosa*, has loose tufts of pale green, grass-like leaves, up to 30 centimetres long, and leafless branching flower stems 50–60 centimetres tall. The blue flowers, with 6 segments and prominent yellow stamens, appear in late spring, followed by three-sided capsules which, when dry, split to release the black seeds. The blue lily prefers a damp situation.

The nodding blue lily, *S. glauca*, is more often found on poor stony soil. It has upright or sprawling slender stems with long narrow, greyish-green leaves and open heads of bright blue, pendulous starry flowers. The foliage is believed to be poisonous to stock.

The blue tinsel lily, *Calectasia cyanea*, is another native with starry blue flowers and prominent yellow anthers. However, unlike the flax lilies and blue lilies, it is not a clump forming perennial but a small, wiry, heath-like shrub less than 60 centimetres in height. It is found in dry, sandy locations in western Victoria, South Australia and eastern areas of Western Australia.

The swamp lily, *Crinum pendunculatum*, found along the coast of New South Wales and Queensland, favours a cool, damp position. The long white flowers, held on a stem of up to 2 metres, have a spidery appearance.

ANT R & D Keller

The Tasmanian flax lily, *Dianella tasmanica*, is common throughout Tasmania and in cooler areas of Victoria. The mauve and yellow flowers are followed in late summer by deep blue berries 1–2 centimetres long.

ANT I.R. McCann

The flowers of the bulbine lily, *Bulbine bulbosa*, are seen in spring in many areas. When not flowering, the bulbine lily is easily confused with the common onion weed.

ANT O. Rogge

The fringe lilies are easily recognised by their three broad petals, fringed at the edges. They range from clump forming to climbing types, but in all the flowers are very similar.

ANT O. Rogge

ANT I.R. McCann

The black anther lily, *Dianella revoluta,* is widespread along coastal areas from Western Australia to Queensland. The striking purple flowers are borne on stems up to 1 metre in height.

ANT O. Rogge

Unlike most other plants, the twining fringe lily, *Thysanotus patersonii,* photosynthesises in the stems. The basal foliage disappears, leaving only the climbing stem.

ANT Keith Vagg

The chocolate lily, *Dichopogon strictus,* is one of the less conspicuous lilies. Found throughout the temperate areas of Australia, except the arid centre and alps, the chocolate lily has a strong chocolate scent.

ANT Keith Williams

The rush lily, *Sowerbaea juncea,* is found in swamps in Victoria and New South Wales but is becoming increasingly rare in Queensland, where much of its former habitat has been drained for housing.

The bright green, linear leaves are crowded, small (2 centimetres) and sharply pointed. The rich blue or purple, iridescent, papery flowers are about 2.5 centimetres across with 6 long, narrow, pointed segments and 6 bright yellow upright stamens. They appear in late winter in Western Australia but in early spring in more easterly localities.

Onion weed lookalike

The bulbine lily, *Bulbine bulbosa*, and the leek lily, *B. semibarbata*, are very different from the blue tinsel lily. Both are endemic to Australia although there are a number of other species native to South Africa. The bulbine lily is found in many areas and, when not in flower, is easily confused with the pestiferous onion weed as its long, narrow, fleshy leaves springing from its bulbous roots are very similar. The bright yellow starry flowers, with tufts of fine yellow hairs on the stamens, are scattered along the erect flower stalks in spring.

The leek lily is similar in appearance but the individual flower stalks are longer, the flowers more widely spaced on the stem and only three of the six stamens bear tufts of hair. The bulbine lily is usually found in grasslands among rocks while the leek lily occupies a wide variety of habitats.

The various species of fringe lilies, *Thysanotus*, include clump forming and climbing types but are easily recognised as the blue or purple blooms have three broad petals with conspicuously fringed edges. Most flower profusely through spring and summer, one short lived flower closely following another. The common fringe lily, *T. tuberosus*, makes a clump of grass-like greyish leaves from which rise upright, flowering stems about 20 centimetres tall on whose branches are lustrous, purple flowers 2.5 centimetres across. It has a tuberous root system.

The twining fringe lily, *T. patersonii*, soon loses its clump of basal foliage and depends on its leafless climbing stems for photosynthesis. The short side branches bear small violet coloured flowers only 8–10 millimetres across.

Other less conspicuous members of the lily family include the grass lilies, *Caesia*, with their tufts of grassy leaves and white to pale blue or mauve star-shaped flowers on slender stems; the strongly-scented vanilla lilies, *Arthropodium*, with spikes of pale blue or white, 6 segmented flowers, and the similar chocolate lilies, *Dichopogon*, whose little flowers are mauve or white.

Some plants although commonly called lilies, such as rock lilies, *Dendrobium speciosum*, water lilies, *Nelumbo* and *Nymphaea*, swamp lilies, *Ottelia*, and Helmholtzia lilies, *Helmholtzia*, are not closely related to the lily family and have been discussed elsewhere. ●

BORONIAS

Characteristic fragrance of spring

In spring the scent of boronias in the air is part of the characteristic fragrance of the Australian bush. There are about 80 known species of the genus *Boronia*. These are shrubby, evergreen plants endemic to Australia but named after an Italian, Francesco Borone, by his friend, the English botanist, James Edward Smith. Borone, also a botanist, died while still a young man when he fell from a window in Athens. In 1798, Smith, who was the founder of the Linnaean Society, immortalised his name by giving it to the first four boronias collected in the Port Jackson area.

The highly perfumed *Boronia megastigma lutea*.

Dwarf boronia, *B. nana* var. *hyssopifolia,* a native of south-eastern Australia. A small, compact plant, it prefers a fairly dry climate as long as its roots are shaded.

ANT G. Cheers

Another of the dwarf boronia, var. *pubescens,* this boronia is widespread throughout southern Australia. It is common in sclerophyll forests where sufficient light penetrates the canopy.

ANT I.R. McCann

Bronzy boronia, *B. thujona,* is a small shrub growing to about 1 metre. It is fairly common in heathland areas along the New South Wales coast. Bronzy boronia is a favourite with the multitude of insects along the coast, attracted by its scent.

ANT I.R. McCann

Found in the moister areas of New South Wales, Victoria and Tasmania, the well-known pink boronia, *B. muelleri,* grows to between one and three metres. It is less compact than many of its relatives, but its floral display is no less spectacular.

ANT I.R. McCann

Generally, boronias are found in heathlands or dry sclerophyll forest where there is shade from other plants, and the leaf mulch keeps the soil at a constant temperature. Their form varies. Most are bushes, one metre or less tall. There are also prostrate forms like *B. polygalifolia,* which spreads almost unnoticed on the floor of the eucalypt forests of coastal New South Wales, and *B. nana,* widespread in the eastern states and South Australia, which rarely reaches more than 15 centimetres in height, as well as very large species such as the bronzy boronia, *B. thujona,* a large shrub up to four metres tall, and the variable pink boronia, *B. muelleri,* which in favourable conditions on rich mountain soils becomes a small tree five to six metres in height.

The pungent stinkwood

Some boronias have simple leaves; in others the foliage is divided into leaflets. Very often it is pleasantly aromatic when crushed although occasionally, as in the stinkwood, *B. variabilis,* of King and Flinders Islands, it is pungent and disagreeable. Boronia flowers have four parts. This makes them easy to distinguish from *Crowea* and *Eriostemon* flowers which have five petals. The petals may be rounded or pointed, wide open, making a starry flower, or curled in to form cup- or bell-shaped blooms. The eight stamens curve inwards forming a cage-like structure around the central style. The colours range from white, through various shades of pink, and red and lilac-blue, to yellow and brown.

Extracting the perfume

In a number of boronias the flowers as well as the foliage are perfumed. Attempts were made in the early days to extract its perfume for commercial use, but this proved to be very difficult until 1924 when a new method using volatile solvents was tried and found successful. Boronia oil was then produced commercially from brown boronia but, by the 1950s, growers preferred to sell their blooms as fresh flowers, this being economically more rewarding. Some boronias, like the brown boronia, have a distinctive perfume not found in other plants but some tend to smell like lemons, myrtle or even black currants.

More than half of the boronia species are native to Western Australia but some of these are extensively grown in the eastern states. The best known of all species, brown boronia, is one of these. It is a rather open rounded shrub, about one metre tall, which grows naturally in swampy patches of the jarrah forests in the south west of Western Australia. Like a number of other boronias, it is short lived. The dark-green aromatic divided leaves are composed of tiny, needle-like leaflets, and the small strongly perfumed cup-shaped flowers, which hang down along the stems, are brown outside and yellow within. There are pure yellow forms. Like most other species the brown boronia flowers in early spring or, sometimes, in late winter. Strangely its fragrance cannot be detected by some people.

The native rose

Another strongly scented species, the native rose, *B. serrulata*, bears little resemblance to the brown boronia. Its native habitat covers the sandstone ridges of the central coast of New South Wales from Gosford to the Royal National Park and west to the foothills of the Blue Mountains. It makes an upright shrub, about 1m in height, the stems crowded with bright green, aromatic, rhomboid leaves whose finely toothed margins are tinged with red. In spring, small clusters of fragrant bright pink, cup-shaped flowers, about 1 centimetre across, appear on the tips of the branches.

The red boronia

The red or Kalgan boronia, *B. heterophylla*, is, like the brown boronia, a native of Western Australia but it is a sturdier bush over one metre tall. It is also longer-lived, often lasting for more than 20 years. The dark green leaves, coarser and larger than those of the brown boronia, may be long and narrow, up to 3.5 centimetres long and three millimetres wide, or divided into long narrow leaflets. This variability is recognised in the species name, *hetero* — different and *phylla* — leaves. The bright pink flowers, hanging bell-like along the stems, are more lightly scented than their brown relatives and, as in many other species, the shade of pink can differ from bush to bush.

Three species frequently seen on the sandstone ridges of coastal New South Wales are the pale pink or flowery boronia, *B. floribunda*, the feather-leafed boronia, *B. pinnata*, and the Sydney boronia, *B. ledifolia*. The pale pink boronia makes an open shrub, one metre or so in height, with divided ferny, light green foliage which is aromatic when bruised. The main leaf stalk is winged. In spring it is massed with large, pale pink, starry flowers, faintly perfumed. The feather-leafed boronia, which also grows in Queensland, has similar fern-like foliage but the central leaf stem is not winged. The fragrance in the leaves is not as generally appreciated as that of some other boronias. The lightly scented starry flowers, opening in spring, are most commonly light pink but may be white or pale mauve. It is one of the longer-lived species. The Sydney boronia spreads into eastern Victoria. It is an upright shrub, often bigger than the other two, with variable leaves which may be simple and lance-shaped, up to 3.5 centimetres long and 10 millimetres wide, or they may have a pair of

One of the favourites of Australian gardeners, brown boronia, *B. megastigma,* is a native of Western Australia. In the wild it prefers moist, but not wet, soil — conditions many gardeners fail to reproduce. Too much moisture invariably results in root rot.

The red boronia, *B. heterophylla,* is another native of Western Australia but is much sturdier than the brown boronia. The scent is quite delicate, and the flower colour varies somewhat according to local conditions.

The alpine boronia, *B. algida,* is found throughout the highland areas of south-eastern Australia. On Mount Hotham and the Bogong High Plains it is fairly common and quite easy to spot among the low, wind-blown vegetation.

A close-up look at the brown boronia flower. Note the perfect symmetry and delicate blending of browns and yellow.

boronia, *B. algida* and the lemon scented boronia, *B. citriodora*. The alpine boronia is a low compact shrub which grows in the Victorian Alps and the Snowy Mountains of New South Wales. The shining dark green leaves are composed of five small, almost circular, leaflets which release a strong scent when bruised. The starry flowers, pink in the bud but opening to almost white, are small, 8–12 millimetres across, and appear in early summer. The lemon-scented boronia, also flowering in early summer, is an even smaller shrub, less than 60 centimetres tall, with thick dark green divided leaves smelling strongly of lemons when crushed. The open, star-like flowers are palest pink. It grows from the subalpine stretches to sea-level in south western Tasmania.

A boronia which flourishes in very different conditions from either coastal or cool montane sites is the sandstone boronia, *B. glabra*, one of those species akin to the Sydney boronia. Its range extends through the north and central western slopes of New South Wales into Queensland. It is one of the taller-growing boronias, sometimes reaching 2.5 metres in height, although it can be much smaller. Its long narrow leaves with their blunt rounded tips are undivided, and it has deep pink starry flowers which open in the spring.

Intermittent blooms

While most boronias flower for a few weeks, usually in spring or perhaps into summer, a few bloom intermittently through the year. The little sickle or wallum boronia, *B. falcifolia*, is common in the swampy, coastal stretches from northern New South Wales up the coast of Queensland. It is a dense erect shrub, generally about 50 centimetres tall, with divided leaves whose leaflets are pointed and needle-like. The broad-petalled, open flowers appear in all seasons. The swamp boronia, *B. parviflora*, is another small plant whose habitat is the swamp lands from Queensland south to Tasmania and South Australia. Its leaves are narrowly elliptical and the small pink flowers have pink sepals almost as large as the petals. It blooms throughout the year.

With the exception of the brown boronia, the species mentioned so far have flower colours ranging from white to deep pink or red, but some forms of the blue boronia, *B. coerulescens*, have lilac-coloured flowers which turn much bluer as they mature. The petals are rounded, opening out into a bloom 1.5 centimetres across. The bush is small and sparse, less than 50 centimetres tall, with short, thick, very narrow leaves only about 7 millimetres long. It is widespread in New South Wales, Victoria, South Australia and Western Australia, where it grows best in dry sandy spots like the mallee scrub. ●

small leaflets at the base. They have a rather unpleasant smell when crushed. The open, bright pink flowers are seen from late winter into spring. There are a number of very similar species.

The Victorian von Muelleri's or tree boronia, *B. muelleri*, is similar to the feather-leafed boronia but the leaflets are narrower and the flowers, differing in botanical detail, are smaller. It prefers damp and shaded gullies where it is reported to reach six metres in height.

Boronias on the alpine reaches

Two boronias thriving in quite different conditions from those so far described are the alpine

The coast boronia, *B. safrolifera,* is a native of northern New South Wales and southern Queensland. Its survival is threatened in many areas because of coastal development.

ANT Keith Williams

PAPERBARK PLANTS

A group of tough shrubs, survivors in many inhospitable climates and conditions

Paperbarks have long been among Australia's most distinctive and useful native plants, easily surviving in rough conditions, even in polluted areas. Until recent times some Aboriginal women around the Northern Territory used paperbark to cover their heads when seen in public; today products of this versatile plant are used in boatbuilding, garden furniture and the chemical industry.

Most paperbarks are recognised by the papery, continuously peeling bark which hangs in thin layers on their trunks and branches. These remarkably hardy trees are characteristic of swampy, poorly drained, brackish soils throughout Australia.

The mauve flowers of *M. thymifolia* appear mostly in summer although some clones in milder climates produce flowers all year.

The snowstorm, *M. linarifolia*, is a well-known tree and a profuse flowerer. It grows to 1.5 metres and is fully developed in 6 years.

The Western Australian, *M. elliptica*, is an attractive shrub which grows large, red, bottle-brush like spikes in spring, summer and autumn.

The flaky peeling bark of paperbark trees (far left) protects the trunk from temperature variations and water loss. The deep mauve flowers of the shrub *M. conothamnoides* (inset) occur in spring.

A tree which grows to 25 metres, the *M. quinquenervia* produces cream-coloured cylindrical spikes.

While some grow well in water, others may be found on dry limestone formations far from water, or on inland sand plains. Their ability to survive in conditions which are unfavourable to the majority of other plants often results in their occurrence in pure stands, particularly in swamps and along the banks of streams and lagoons.

The name 'paperbark' refers to a large group of shrubs and trees up to 30 metres high which belong to the genus *Melaleuca*, its 140 or so species being mostly native to Australia, with several from New Guinea, the Malay Archipelago and New Caledonia.

The name of the genus comes from the Greek '*melas*' meaning black and '*leukos*', white, probably referring to the fact that the first paperbark discovered had white branches but a black trunk, possibly from fire. Alternatively, it could be a reference to the mottled dark and light colouring of the bark of some species.

Closely related to *Callistemon* (bottlebrush) trees and shrubs, melaleucas have very similar brush-like flowers and this often causes some confusion. However, a closer examination reveals a distinct difference: the very long, colourful stamens of the paperbarks are united in bundles, whereas those of the bottlebrushes grow freely.

Both paperbarks and bottlebrushes belong to the widely distributed myrtle family (Myrtaceae) which has many representatives in the Southern Hemisphere and a few in northern countries. The flowers of paperbarks create dazzling spring and summer displays, in colours including white, cream, pink, mauve, scarlet and orange depending on species.

Dead cells protect life

The bark of melaleucas, varying in colour from grey, brown or cream to vivid white, is usually papery in consistency, although in some species it is hard and furrowed. The flaky, peeling bark characterising the majority of paperbarks consists of layers of dead cells which form outside the living bark to protect the trunk from temperature variations and water loss.

This enables the trees to withstand climatic extremes and salt-laden winds. As the tree develops, the layers of dead cells cannot grow with it and so they become partially separated from the trunk in flaky sheets.

The tough, resilient qualities of this bark have made it extremely useful, in the past to bush-dwellers and more recently, to those living in cities.

Early European settlers used it for bedding and for thousands of years Aboriginals have employed it for a variety of purposes, such as providing cover for their shelters and material for wrapping food and other objects. The thick, papery bark of the broad-leafed paperbark

The dense upright shrub, *M. diosmifolia*, bears light green bottle-brush like spikes in summer.

Native to Western Australia, the shrub *M. nematophylla* bears large, globular purple flowers in spring and summer.

The claw flower, *M. pulchella*, is an attractive shrub with cascading branches. Its exquisite flowers appear in spring and summer.

The large white, mauve or purple flowers of *M. radula* appear in small clusters in spring and summer.

Bay Picture Library

(*Melaleuca quinquenervia*), abundant in the coastal swamps of eastern Australia, was a species often used.

The swamp paperbark (*M. ericifolia*), an exceptionally hardy species of southeastern Australia with fine, dark green leaves and white flowers, has been particularly useful because of the water-resistant quality of its bark.

Aboriginals used sheets of this bark to construct rough canoes, binding them together with the fibre of the hemp-bush (*Gynatrix pulchella*), and to make water-carrying baskets.

The ability of melaleuca bark to retain water is still appreciated today, small strips being used to line hanging baskets for indoor plants.

Trunk provided water

Aboriginals also obtained water from paperbarks growing near billabongs or swamps. Cutting into a certain flat part of the trunk, they drank the water which trickled from it.

This water was generally salty, and so not particularly enjoyable to drink, but it was naturally welcomed by thirsty wanderers.

As well as these practical functions, it is interesting to note the more spiritual connotations of paperbarks for some Aboriginals.

Until relatively recent times Aboriginal women of Groote Eylandt, off the northeast coast of the Northern Territory, used to cover their heads with paperbark when collecting food and water or performing other necessary outdoor activities during the daylight hours.

Early visitors to the island seldom saw these women, but heard their voices in the bush. The reason for this secrecy was that the women of Groote Eylandt were following the pattern of certain ancestral spirits, a group of women called the Wuradilagu who lived amongst the trees and covered themselves with paperbark wherever they might have been observed.

Used for furniture

Today paperbarks are used throughout Australia for a variety of purposes. Because the timber of most of the tree-size species is unaffected by moisture, it is valuable for posts in wet ground as well as for boatbuilding. Saplings of swamp paperbark are used to make 'rustic' garden furniture and informal 'brushwood' fencing.

Paperbarks are also used extensively for landscaping, particularly some of the larger eastern species such as the prickly-leafed paperbark, *M. styphelioides*, and the ability of many species to tolerate urban pollution and saline soils is a great advantage.

The foliage of paperbarks, which is variable according to species and includes needle-like, flat or scale-like leaves, is in demand for floral art. Two species, *M. alternifolia* and *M. linarifolia*, yield fragrant oils with antiseptic properties which are used in detergents.

DRUMSTICKS AND CONESTICKS

Rock-loving plants with bearded fruits

One of the most spectacular species of drumsticks grows on the high slopes of Western Australia's Stirling Ranges. Heads of bright pink flowers bloom in the spring.

Auscape Int. Jean-Paul Ferrero

Drumsticks, conesticks, conebushes and coneflowers are the common names generally used for two groups of native shrubs, *Isopogon* and *Petrophile*, which have large, knob-like fruits. These names are more obviously appropriate than the literal translations of their botanical names: *Isopogon*, 'isos' – equal and 'pogon' – beard, referring to the hairy fruits of most species, and *Petrophile*, 'petros' – rock and 'philos' – love, referring to the rocky habitats preferred by some species.

Both groups belong to the same family, *Proteaceae*, as the grevilleas, banksias and waratahs. They both include a range of shrubby plants up to 2–3 metres tall with stiff, simple or divided leaves and heads of long, thin, tubular flowers which split into 4 recurving segments at the mouth. The exposed style is thickened near the tip, often brightly and contrastingly coloured. Each flower is supported by a single bract and the heads are either terminal or axillary. The colour range is mostly confined to creams, yellows and pinks.

There are about 32 species of *Isopogon*, all endemic to Australia, of which only 6 are found in the eastern half of the continent, the remainder occuring in Western Australia, mostly in the south-west corner. In the east they are commonly known as drumsticks because of the globular shape of the seed heads of two common species, *I. anemonifolius* and *I. anethifolius*. These are very conspicuous and remain on the bush for a number of years. Other eastern species and those in the west are often called conebushes or coneflowers.

Subtle differences

Although *Isopogon* and *Petrophile* species are similar in so many ways, there are some differences which make field identification possible. In *Isopogon* the flower heads are usually short, crowded cylinders and the bracts at the bases of the flowers are deciduous, either falling with the flowers or remaining to form a smooth, protective, globular cone which disintegrates when the small, rounded nuts are released. The flower heads of *Petrophile* species are more likely to be in spikes and the bracts are persistent, opening to free the flattened nutlets, but remaining attached to the central axis to form a rough, prickly, elongated cone. While the nuts of *Isopogon* tend to be hairy, those of *Petrophile* have long tufts of hairs only on the edges.

Drumstick, *I. anemonifolius*, sometimes called tall conebush, is very common in the heathlands and poor soils of the coastal and tableland forests from eastern Victoria north to the Queensland border. It is usually a fairly upright shrub, 2 metres tall by 1.5 metres across, the stems springing from a thickened rootstock which, by containing a reserve food supply, allows the plant to survive bush fires. The 10 centimetre light green leaves are widely divided into narrow, stiff, flattened segments tending to curl upwards. In cold weather the foliage turns greenish-purple. In spring the terminal yellow flowerheads begin to open and by autumn they will have been replaced by the smooth, grey, rounded cones 2–3 centimetres across from which the plant takes its common name.

Another drumstick, *I. anethifolius*, is found only in the coastal plains and Blue Mountains of New South Wales. It is a dense, upright shrub, sometimes reaching 3 metres, with reddish, young stems and divided leaves, up to 16 centimetres long, the segments narrow, tapering and cylindrical. The bright yellow, terminal flowerheads are produced for a long period starting in late spring. The bracts have dark, projecting, pointed tips.

Flowers half hidden

The horny conebush, *I. ceratophyllus*, is widespread in the east, growing in South Australia,

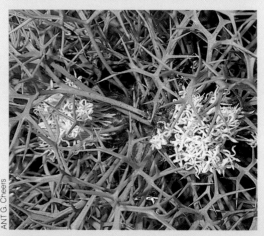

Common in eastern Australia, these drumsticks have prominent heads of yellow flowers. They grow on a spreading shrub which reaches about two metres in height.

Found only in the coastal plains and Blue Mountains region of New South Wales, this sturdy drumstick bears prominent heads of yellow flowers in spring and early summer.

The thorny conebush is a low, prickly shrub. Its light green foliage is dense and rigid and its flowers appear in spring and throughout the year.

The rose coneflower is a Western Australian species common in the woodlands north of Albany (below). Its leaves are deeply divided into pointed, cylindrical segments.

The pincushion coneflower is another pink-flowered Western Australian species (above). The large, terminal flowers have woolly bracts and flowers appear in late winter and early spring.

The pale, hairy coneflower is frequently seen in the jarrah forests, north and south of Perth. This shrubby bush grows to about 1.5 metres tall.

The prickly conestick is an upright shrub found in the sandstone hills of eastern New South Wales and Queensland. Its pale, creamy flowers occur on terminal spikes which are covered in down.

The granite petrophile is a straggling, upright shrub with sharply pointed, divided leaves. Found in an area east of Perth, this plant is covered with blossoms in winter and spring.

Victoria, New South Wales and Tasmania. It is quite different from those already described, being a low, spreading, prickly shrub no more than 60 centimetres tall but covering an area 1.2 metres across. The light green foliage is dense and rigid and the upright tufts of yellow flowers are half hidden among the divided leaves. The flowers appear in spring and intermittently through the year. The fruiting heads are the typical, smooth, grey-brown knobs.

One of the most spectacular species, the Western Australian *I. latifolius*, is found in the high parts of the Stirling Range far to the south of that State. In late spring it bears large, terminal heads of bright pink flowers up to 8 centimetres across. The shrub is rounded, about 2 metres tall and has light green, elliptical, undivided leaves up to 10 centimetres long.

Other pink-flowered, Western Australian species include the rose coneflower, *I. formosus*, the pincushion coneflower, *I. dubius* (syn. *I. roseus*) and the pale, hairy Stirling Range coneflower, *I. baxteri*. The rose coneflower, a rounded shrub to 1.5 metres tall, has its leaves deeply divided into pointed, cylindrical segments. The large, terminal flowerheads have woolly bracts and when the pink flowers open in late winter and early spring, the heads measure 4–6 centimetres across. It is common in the woodlands north of Albany.

Mop-like blooms

From mid-winter into spring the pincushion coneflower has rather moplike, terminal heads of deep pink, silky flowers measuring up to 5 centimetres across. The short bracts are covered with small hairs. The leaves are divided, and the segments narrow, channelled and sharply pointed. The pincushion coneflower is a small shrub, up to 1 metre tall, and is frequently seen in the jarrah forests north and east of Perth.

The Stirling Range coneflower has tufts of very soft pink flowers covered in fine hairs, giving the effect of a bunch of long, narrow feathers. The projecting styles are deep orange. The reddish stems are lightly dusted with hairs and the 2–3 centimetre, wedge-shaped leaves have prickly, pointed lobes. The leaves of the nodding coneflower, *I. teretifolius*, may be either simple or divided into cylindrical segments. The shrub grows in open heaths in the far south of Western Australia, making a small stiff plant no more than 1 metre tall. The flowers are pale pink and, as the coloquial name implies, are often turned down.

Of the 40 odd species of *Petrophile*, all endemic to Australia, the majority are restricted to the south-west corner of the continent and only 5 species grow in the eastern half. None of these occur in Victoria or Tasmania. Generally the flowerheads make a tubular spike and the fruit-

Auscape International Graeme Chapman

Auscape Int. Colin Totterdell.

Auscape International Graeme Chapman

Bay Picture Library

Bay Picture Library

ANT I. McCann

ing heads are elongated, rather than rounded cones.

Prefers poor soil

The prickly conesticks, *P. canescens* (syn. *P. sessilis*) is an open, upright shrub, sometimes reaching 3 metres, which is common on the poor sandstone hills of eastern New South Wales and Queensland. The 10 centimetre leaves are divided into widely spaced, narrow segments and the pale, creamy spring and summer flowers in 5 centimetre terminal spikes, are covered with down, and the stalkless cones oval-shaped.

Stalked conesticks, *P. pedunculata*, is another sparse, erect shrub about 2.5 metres tall which is seen mostly on coastal regions of northern New South Wales and the south-east corner of Queensland. The dark green, 16 centimetre leaves are divided and the creamy, yellow spikes of flowers, most often in the upper leaf axils, appear in summer. The prominent cones are stalked.

The granite petrophile of Western Australia, *P. biloba*, is covered with sprays of blossoms in winter and spring. The small clusters of pink flowers in the leaf axils are thickly coated with woolly grey hairs and the swollen ends of the projecting styles are bright yellow. The granite petrophile is a rather straggling, upright shrub 1.5–2 metres tall, with sharply pointed, divided leaves. It grows in a small area to the east of Perth.

Low-growing species

A prostrate species, the long-leaved petrophile, *P. longifolia*, is another Western Australian occurring to the north of Albany. Seldom more than 50 centimetres tall, it has short stems with 20–40 centimetre long, narrow, needle-like leaves held vertically. The silky flowerheads, soft yellow tinged with brown, nestle down among the foliage from October to January.

Another small Western Australian species, the narrow-leaf conestick, *P. linearis*, is widespread on the west coast north and south of Perth. It is a multi-stemmed shrub, only about 50 centimetres tall, with thick, sickle-shaped leaves, 5–8 centimetres long. The terminal heads of soft, woolly, pink flowers, 4–5 centimetres across, opening in spring, give rise to another common name used in the west, pixie mops.

P. phylicoides, which has no generally accepted common name, is an unusual species. Unlike so many other *Petrophile* the yellow flowers are smooth, not woolly or hairy and the lobes at the tips of the flower tubes carry small, pointed projections. It grows on the south coast of Western Australia. The terminal flowerheads, which appear in late spring, are carried on stems clothed with deep-green, 1 centimetre long, needle-like leaves.

As with so many native plants the western species of both drumsticks and conesticks are difficult to cultivate in the eastern States but *I. anemonifolius* and *I. anethifolius* are hardy plants, growing easily in sunny, well-drained positions and *P. pedunculata* responds to suitable conditions.

The narrow leaf conestick is widespread on the coast, north and south of Perth (top left). The terminal heads of pink flowers have given it the common name of pixie mops.

Western Australia has a number of pincushion coneflower varieties (above). All grow on an erect, prickly shrub which grow to about 60 centimetres high with divided leaves.

KANGAROO PAWS

*One species has reached fame on stamps and as
Western Australia's floral emblem*

Kangaroo paws are neither kangaroos nor paws but brilliantly coloured flowers which grow, in the wild, only in a small corner of Western Australia. In the eastern States many gardens feature kangaroo paws, their colour and size varying a great deal.

Of the numerous plants unique to Western Australia, the kangaroo paw is perhaps the strangest: the tubular flowers, covered with soft, velvety hairs, resemble the animal paw for which they were named.

Their natural habitat is in the southwest corner of Western Australia and along the coastal plains north of Perth to Shark Bay, where well drained, sandy plains, forests and woodlands, heaths and swamps offer the right terrain.

Varying in height from 30 centimetres up to three metres, kangaroo paws form clumps of strap-like leaves from which the flower stalks emerge.

The flowering season varies according to the species but is mostly in the warmer months. Except for the black kangaroo paw, *Macropidia fuliginosa*, the nine or ten known species form a small genus, *Anigozanthos*; all are endemic to Western Australia.

The two genera differ only in the size and number of seeds in the cells of the seed capsules and both are closely related to the cottonheads, *Conostylis*, whose flowers are also covered with fine, woolly hairs.

The kangaroo paw has distinctive narrow, tubular flowers covered with soft, velvety hairs. This species, *A. rufus* is endemic to the Esperance area of W.A.

Bay Picture Library

The golden kangaroo paw, *A. pulcherrimus* grows in sandy heathland on the coast of W.A. as far north as Shark Bay.

The striking green and red kangaroo paw, *A. manglesii* is the floral emblem of W.A. It flowers in spring and is common in bushland around Perth.

A. flavidus grows vigorously in swampy regions of the southwest. It is extremely hardy and is easily cultivated.

The stems and flowers of the black kangaroo paw, *Macropidia fuliginosa* are thickly covered with black hairs. It prefers positions on gravelly, well-drained hills.

Fine hair cover

The long, narrow, tubular flowers split along one side near the tip, opening out into six pointed segments. This characteristic gives the genus its botanical name, *Anigozanthos*, which comes from the Greek words *anoigo*, 'expanded' and *anthos*, 'flower'. The flowers and the long, sturdy flower stems are thickly covered with fine hairs which, particularly in *A. rufus* where they are reddish-brown, give the young flower heads a fancied resemblance to the foot of a kangaroo. The yellow flowered *A. humilis* is generally called the cat's paw, perhaps because the spreading segments of the down-turned flower are so like the grasping paws of a cat as it catches its prey.

Flower colours range through red, orange and yellow to brilliant green, often combined and extending down the long flower stems. Even within one species variations in colour may occur. The fine hairs covering both flowers and stems can either match the flower colour or contrast with it, as in the case of the black kangaroo paw, where the greeny-yellow colour of the blooms is almost hidden by jet black hairs.

Probably the most widely known of all the species is the green and red kangaroo paw, *A. manglesii*, which is common in the bushland around Perth and grows freely on the sand plains from Geraldton to Albany. This striking plant produces its crest-like heads of brilliant green flowers, each 6–7 centimetres long, on thickly furred, crimson stems up a metre in height in winter and spring.

It has been adopted as the floral emblem of the State and is also depicted on Australian stamps. Although not the first of the kangaroo paws to be cultivated in the Northern Hemisphere, within five years of the settlement of the Swan River Colony, as Perth was originally known, Governor James Stirling had sent seeds of the red and green kangaroo paw to England. They were successfully raised in 1833 in the Berkshire garden of Robert Mangels whose name was later given to the plant.

Found in swampy areas

Twice as tall as the green and red kangaroo paw, *A. flavidus*, sometimes called the tree kangaroo paw, is a very hardy species found in the swampy areas of the extreme south-west where it makes large clumps up to a metre or more across. The late spring and summer flowers, only half the length of those of the red and green variety, are mostly muddy yellow with a tinge of red but are sometimes seen in brighter pinks, reds and greens. While not as brilliantly coloured as other species, it is easily cultivated and grows vigorously.

The cat's paw, *A. humilis* is often cultivated in suburban gardens where it prefers sandy soil, full sun and a minimum of watering.

North of Perth, the yellow form of the cat's paw dominates while in the south and east, the orange-red forms are seen.

Many species of honey-eating birds, including this New Holland honeyeater are attracted to the kangaroo paw which is rich in nectar.

Mangels kangaroo paw was named after Robert Mangel who successfully grew the plant in his English garden in 1833 from seeds sent from Governor Stirling in Perth.

Other eye-catching species include the spring-flowering green kangaroo paw, *A. viridis*, found also in swampy areas. It has narrow, almost tube-like foliage and flower stems only 40–50 centimetres tall, and the flowers vary from bright, clear yellow to sharp, forest green in colour.

The golden kangaroo paw, *A. pulcherrimus*, growing in sandy heathland on the west coast as far north as Shark Bay, has greyish leaves and branching flower stems up to a metre or more in height carrying vibrant yellow flowers from late spring to autumn. Unfortunately, this is one of the more difficult species to grow.

The black kangaroo paw also grows on the west coast but prefers a drier position and is usually found on gravelly, well-drained hills. The branching stems and yellow-green flowers, thickly covered with black hairs, emerge from clumps of flattened leaves up to 50 centimetres in height.

When specimens were sent to Europe by the government botanist James Drummond, he referred to it as 'a real mourning flower'. Unfortunately this bizarre plant is almost impossible to cultivate from seed, and even successful division of the clump is extremely difficult, and so it's rare outside its natural habitat.

Nectar attracts birds

Kangaroo paws are rich in nectar, attracting many honey-eating birds including the New Holland honeyeater, sometimes called the watchdog of the bush, as it chatters loudly at the sight of an intruder.

The tiny western spinebill, *Acanthorhynchus superciliosus*, not only feeds on the nectar but is also an important pollinating agent. As it hovers in front of the flowers like the humming birds of South America, it thrusts its long, curved bill into the tube of the blossom and in doing so brushes its head against the pollen sacs at the mouth of the tube, transferring the pollen between the flowers it visits.

This little bird is found only in Western Australia but its cousin, the eastern spinebill, *A. tenuriostris*, now provides the same service to cultivated kangaroo paws in the eastern States.

Because of the interest shown in the cultivation of these native plants both for the garden and the cut flower trade, research into growing them has been carried on for some years in the National Botanic Gardens, Canberra, and also by individuals.

Attempts at hybridising to produce improved colour combined with the vigour of the tree kangaroo paw have met with some success and one chance cultivar, 'Pink Joey' has been registered. ●

BEAUTIFUL BOTTLEBRUSHES

Easy to grow, easy to love

The spectacular gold-tipped bottlebrush, *C. polandii*, found in sclerophyll forests of north Queensland.

ANT Keith Williams

Bottlebrushes, among the most popular native plants cultivated as ornamentals, are endemic to Australia and contain about 25 recognised species as well as many varieties and cultivars. They are easily grown, hardy, adaptable and, when in flower, are well described by their botanical name *Callistemon* which is derived from the Greek, 'kallistos' — most beautiful and 'stemon' — stamens. The individual flowers are small with inconspicuous, greenish, deciduous sepals and petals surrounding a number of long stamens but when the flowers are massed together in terminal spikes they form conspicuous, cylindrical brush-like flowerheads.

The long stamens are often brightly coloured and tipped with golden anthers. Many of the species have flowers in shades of pink or red but they may also be white, yellow, green or mauve, the cultivated plants extending the range even further. They all attract bees and small birds.

Other native plants with similar flower spikes are the tea-trees, *Melaleuca*, and net bushes, *Calothamnus*. While the stamens of the bottlebrushes are free, those of the tea-trees are fused into five distinct bundles and those of the net bushes united into flattened groups. The flowers which usually open in spring and summer are followed by three-celled woody capsules filled with minute seeds. The capsules are packed together along the central stem and remain on the plant for an indefinite period, usually years.

In some species the seed is released when ripe, in others it is only freed when the branch dies. The tip of the flower spike grows on into a new shoot which will in its turn produce a new flower, to be followed by seed capsules and a further new shoot. Bottlebrush leaves, which are arranged alternately along the stems, are simple, usually long, narrow and flat with smooth edges. Many are dull green but some species have pink, red or fresh green young growth in spring.

The willow bottlebrush is one of the largest species, reaching up to 10 metres in height. The creamy-white flowers appear in spring, sometimes carrying over into early summer. The willow bottlebrush prefers a moist location, with full sun.

ANT Keith Williams

The brilliant red blooms of the crimson bottlebrush appear in early summer, and then again in autumn. Like many of the bottlebrushes, it is a tolerant species, even adapting to overly-moist ground.

Jean-Paul Ferrero

A variable species with regard to height, the alpine bottlebrush ranges between 1 and 4 metres. Despite its specific habitat requirements — cold areas between 900 and 2000 metres and swampy ground — it still does quite well in gardens and rockeries.

ANT I.R. McCann

The lemon bottlebrush is a hardy species found throughout the south-east of Australia, including Tasmania. Unlike many species, the seed capsules are spaced out along the stem, not crowded into a mass.

ANT G. Cheers

Callistemon 'Mauve Mist', one of the many cultivars available, originated from another cultivar, 'Reeve's Pink', which in turn was developed from *C. citrinus*. The mauve-pink flowers of 'Mauve Mist' are produced in summer, and the bush measuring only 3 metres by 3 metres, makes a useful addition to almost any garden.

Callistemon 'Captain Cook', a dwarf cultivar of *C. viminalis*, gained widespread acceptance among gardeners when it first appeared on the market. It has all the beauty of the parent plant, which grows to about 10 metres, but none of its size — 'Captain Cook' reaches only 1–1.5 metres.

Typical of the Western Australian species of bottlebrush, western glory carries fiery-red flower heads over a long period. It has proven quite useful in cultivation, especially in 'low maintainance' gardens for, once established, it is fairly tolerant of dry conditions.

Callistemon 'Endeavour' is another cultivar of *C. citrinus*, appropriately named as a follow-up release to 'Captain Cook'. The two complement one another perfectly, 'Endeavour' being somewhat taller, with less of a weeping tendency.

Creamy flowers

The growth habit of most bottlebrushes is shrubby but a few grow into small trees reaching perhaps to 10 metres. One of these, the white or willow bottlebrush, *Callistemon salignus*, has bright pink, silky haired young leaves, papery bark and creamy flowers in spring. The mature leaves may be 10 cm long and 1.0–1.5 cm wide, leathery and dark green. The willow bottlebrush grows freely in moist locations from south-east Queensland to the western slopes and south coast of New South Wales.

Another of the tree-like *Callistemon* is the well-known weeping bottlebrush, *C. viminalis*. Its habitat is the coastal stretches of southern Queensland and northern New South Wales where it grows along the river banks. A well grown tree may reach 10 metres or more with a rounded head and pendulous branches.

The leaves are slightly narrower than those of the willow bottlebrush and covered with aromatic oil glands. The red brushes vary from 4–10 cm in length and are carried most abundantly in spring but intermittently through the rest of the year, often appearing after good rains.

Long flowering

Like the weeping bottlebrush, the crimson bottlebrush, *C. citrinus* (syn. *C. lanceolatus*) has an extended flowering period. The deep red flower spikes, up to 10 cm long and 4–5 cm across, are borne in profusion through October and November and again in the autumn. White forms are occasionally seen.

The crimson bottlebrush makes a large, stiff shrub, 3–4 metres tall and the pointed leaves, which may be 7 cm long and 1.5–2 cm broad, are aromatic when bruised.

It is widespread through most of eastern Australia from central Queensland southwards, usually in moist areas of the coastal plains or foothills of the mountains.

The seeds of this bottlebrush do not always grow true to type and have produced some fine cultivars whose flower colours include deep pink and mauve as well as crimson.

Prefers heights

The alpine bottlebrush, *C. sieberi*, as its name implies, belongs to more elevated regions, growing in swampy areas at altitudes of 900–2000 metres. At the upper end of its range it makes a dense shrub about 1 metre in height but lower down, in more sheltered spots, it may be four times that size.

The leaves are stiff, needle-like and, when young, covered with silky hairs. Although the rich creamy flower spikes are comparatively short, they cover the bushes in late spring at low altitudes and in summer higher up.

Most of the bottlebrush species are found in the eastern States and South Australia but some, like the yellow bottlebrush, *C. pallidus* and the green bottlebrush, *C. viridiflorus*, grow naturally in Tasmania and two, the fiery bottlebrush, *C. phoeniceus* and the Albany or showy bottlebrush, *C. speciosus*, are endemic to Western Australia.

Pale yellow flower

The yellow bottlebrush is an upright shrub, 2–3 metres tall, with almost elliptical leaves, pinkish and silky-haired when young. The pale yellow, rather sparse, flower spikes appear in late spring or summer. The seed capsules are scattered, not crowded, on the stem. It grows in Victoria and New South Wales as well as Tasmania and would not be classed with the showy bottlebrushes.

The green bottlebrush, found naturally only in Tasmania, has stiff, dark green leaves only 2 cm long and makes an erect shrub 2 metres or less in height. It is summer flowering with comparatively short yellowish-green brushes.

The Western Australian species are much more spectacular with strongly coloured, large flowerheads. The fiery bottlebrush grows on the west coast making a shrub 2–3 metres tall and almost as wide. The narrow, grey-green leaves make a good background for the dense spikes of brilliant fiery-red flowers, 10–14 cm long, in late spring and early summer. The closely related Albany bottlebrush is found in swampy regions on the south-west coast. It is a more open shrub with larger, dark green leaves, 10–12 cm long. The flowerheads are deep crimson, sometimes 15 cm long and 5 or 6 cm wide. They appear in spring but may continue intermittently through summer and autumn.

Damp conditions

Another of the red-flowered bottlebrushes common in the coastal regions of south-east Queensland and northern New South Wales, the smooth bottlebrush, *C. pachyphyllus*, has smooth, leathery, blue-green leaves which may be 4–13 cm long and 5–10 cm across. It rarely grows more than 2 metres tall. The flower heads are normally deep red but occasionally white flowered forms are seen.

Most bottlebrushes, while tolerating drier conditions when cultivated, prefer damp situations. One exception is the prickly bottlebrush, *C. brachycandrus*, which forms rounded shrubs about 3 metres high throughout the dry areas of South Australia, Victoria and New South Wales. The sharply pointed needle-like leaves are short, only about 4 cm long and the equally short red brushes appear in summer.

Callistemon 'King's Park Special' is a cultivar of largely unknown origin. It is thought that it originated in King's Park, Perth, probably from species from the eastern states. Whatever its parentage, 'King's Park' is undoubtedly an attractive large shrub or small tree, with a diameter of 3–4 metres.

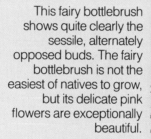

This fairy bottlebrush shows quite clearly the sessile, alternately opposed buds. The fairy bottlebrush is not the easiest of natives to grow, but its delicate pink flowers are exceptionally beautiful.

The paperbark bottlebrush, *C. formosus*, is a pendulous shrub that reaches about 3 metres in height. It occurs naturally along creek banks and in hardwood forests in south-east Queensland. The pale yellow flowers, about 7cm long, can be seen throughout the year.

The Baroondah bottlebrush, a gorgeous pink-flowering tree to 5 metres, takes its name from the site of its first discovery, the Baroondah homestead near Taroom, Queensland. As yet it has not been given a specific Latin name, but it is already grown in cultivation.

THE GROUND ORCHIDS

Mysterious and beautiful

A.N.T. Keith Vagg

Greenhood, double tail, flying duck and beardie — the common names of many ground orchids reflect the curious, sometimes grotesque, shapes of the flowers but not their delicate beauty.

The orchids in many florists' shops are often exotic hybrids grown for their large, eye-catching blooms, but there is enormous variety in native Australian orchids, many of which are rarely seen outside their natural habitats. The dainty and sometimes oddly-shaped flowers are often sweetly scented, a characteristic unusual among exotic species, and may be solitary or massed on long spikes. The waxy petals vary enormously in shape, while colours range from delicate pastel pink, cream, yellow and green to a rare vibrant blue or a deep maroon.

Considered the largest, and by most botanists the most highly developed, of the flowering plant families, the orchid family is extremely widespread, covering most of the globe except for the polar regions, mountain tops and desert areas. Of the 700 or so genera in the family about 70 grow in Australia, but only a handful, such as the hammer orchids of Western Australia and the waxlips of the eastern states, are endemic.

The veined helmet orchid depicts the triffid qualities of the orchid family. It grows in all states except Queensland in moist, cool, sheltered places. *Corybas dilatatus* flowers June to September.

From the temperate south to the arid centre

Terrestrial or ground orchids, which make up the bulk of our 600 or so native species, have typical root systems which draw nourishment and support from the soil. They are most common in the temperate south of Australia. As they do not need a constantly moist atmosphere, one or two, such as species of the greenhoods (*Pterostylis*) and sun orchids (*Thelymitra*), even survive in semi-arid conditions in central Australia; however, others like the swamp lily, *Phaius australis*, thrive in perpetually boggy sites. Ground orchids tolerate a wide variety of soils from sand to clay, and those which do grow on the trunks of tree ferns, on rocks covered with rotting vegetation or in the forks of trees, have extensive roots reaching down into the soil.

Ground orchids use their fleshy roots or underground tubers for storage. Tubers of species including double tails (*Diuris*) and beak orchids (*Lyperanthus*) were sometimes eaten by Aboriginals. The testiculate shape of these tubers gave the name 'orchid' to the family as the Greek word for 'testes' is *orchis*.

Most terrestrial orchids are deciduous, dying in summer, but the scrub lily, *Calanthe triplicata*, swamp lily and Austral ladies tresses, *Spiranthes sinensis*, which grow in boggy sites and rainforests, are evergreen.

In size, ground orchids range from the tiny spurred helmet orchid, *Corybas aconitiflorus*, a scant 3 centimetres in height with a single basal leaf and solitary flower, to the swamp lily, often over two metres in height with sprays of flowers each 10 to 20 centimetres across, and the big clumps of scrub lily whose globular clusters of large white flowers are raised on stems 1.5 metres tall.

Landing platform for insects

Orchids are closely related to lilies: the flowers of each have six floral appendages, three sepals and three petals. These are generally similar in size and shape in lilies, but in most orchids the upper petal, the labellum or lip, is completely different in shape and colour. (Exceptions are the sun orchids whose flower parts are even and regular.) As the bud develops it twists through 180° so that when the flower opens the labellum occupies the central lower position. This is an obvious landing platform for visiting insects, important in pollination.

The male and female organs are fused into one central column directly above the ovary. In most flowers the pollen is a fine loose powder; in orchids it is held together in the column in pairs of mealy clusters, pollinia, each attached to a sticky disc. Although some orchids are self-pollinating (autogamy), most rely on insects to transfer the pollinia from flower to flower. In some species like greenhoods and flying ducks (*Caleana*), once

The potato orchid, *Gastrodia sesamoides* lives on dead and decaying matter. It is usually found where the soil is rich in organic matter.

The common onion orchid, *Microtis unifolia* is widespread along the east coast. It is so called because its thick, short pseudo bulbs resemble onions.

The spotted sun orchid, *Thelmitra ixiodes* grows in all states and is usually blue.

The ruddy greenhood orchid, *Pterostylis rufa* grows in the shade of dense scrub or forest in coastal areas from Victoria to Queensland.

The large tongue orchid (left), sp. *Cryptostylis* attracts the male wasp because its labellum is similar in shape and marking to the female wasp.

The flying duck orchids (left), sp. *Caleana* traps all insects which land on its labellum, using them to transfer its pollinia.

The common donkey orchid (right), *Diuris longifolia* is widespread throughout woodlands. The tubers of this species were sometimes eaten by the Aboriginals.

A.N.T. Otto Rogge

The helmet orchid (left), sp. *Corybas* is one of the smallest of the ground orchids. It is only 3 centimetres in height, has a single leaf and a solitary flower.

Bay Picture Library

The bush lily (right), *Calanthe triplicata* is one of the evergreen orchids which thrive in boggy sites and rainforests.

Bay Picture Library

The streaked rock orchid (left), sp. *Dendrobium* can be seen in rocky areas from Victoria to Queensland.

The widespread hyacinth orchid (right), *Dipodium punctatum* belongs to a group of saprophytes which live in close association with a fungus at its root system.

A.N.T. G Cheers

A.N.T. G&R Wilson

Orchids blooming underground

A small group of ground orchids is saprophytes, plants that are usually leafless and have no chlorophyll to utilise sunlight for growth. They are not parasitic, but live on dead and decaying matter, relying on the help of soil fungi which live within their fleshy roots to absorb nutriment. Saprophytes, including the widespread hyacinth orchid, *Dipodium punctatum*, and the potato orchid, *Gastrodia sesamoides*, are usually found where the soil is rich in organic matter. Other non-saprophytic orchids also enjoy a symbiotic relationship with fungi but not to the same extent.

Strangest of all the saprophytes are the two unique Australian underground orchids. One in Western Australia, *Rhizanthella gardneri*, was turned up by a plough at Carrigin in 1928. The eastern underground orchid, *Cryptanthemis slateri*, was found in 1931 at Bulahdelah in New South Wales. Both live, bloom, and are pollinated underground, the flowers of the eastern variety appearing above the soil when the seeds are ripe for dispersal.

Rare and difficult

Sadly, many orchids are becoming rare as their native habitats are alienated for agriculture or building development. Orchids are protected throughout Australia and may not be dug up or picked in any national park, Crown land or state forest without an official permit (or taken from private land without the permission of the owner). They are increasingly popular with gardeners, although many are difficult, if not impossible, to cultivate under normal garden or greenhouse conditions. Trials of various species are being carried out, with some success, by the National Botanic Gardens in Canberra.

Bay Picture Library

A leafless saprophyte, a hyacinth orchid.

an insect (which may be as small as a mosquito) lands on the lower petal the highly sensitive labellum snaps shut, trapping the insect within the flower. By the time the insect escapes through the back of the flower (or the labellum opens to release it), the sticky disc with the pollinia is attached to the insect's body in precisely the right position to be transferred to the stigma of the next flower.

Bizarre tactics

Some orchids lure insects with droplets of nectar, others resort to more bizarre tactics. The petals and sepals of the tongue orchid (*Cryptostylis*) are narrow and the labellum, which unlike most orchids is at the top, appears somewhat similar in shape and marking to the female ichneumon wasp. The male wasp, attracted to the flower possibly by sight or perhaps by scent, attempts to mate with it thus coming into contact with the sticky disc and its pollinia. Male wasps hatch two weeks before the females and during this time pollinate many flowers. They will even fight for possession of individual blooms, appearing to prefer the bloom to the wingless female wasp.

Thousands of fine seeds are released when the ripe capsules split and are carried long distances by the wind — even, it is believed, as far as New Zealand. But few seeds germinate and it may be several years before plants reach maturity. ●

HIBISCUS

Attractive and edible!

To most gardeners, hibiscus once meant only the Chinese hibiscus, *Hibiscus rosa-sinensis*, and its Hawaiian hybrids, glossy evergreen shrubs with large and brightly coloured flowers, or, in colder climates, the Syrian hibiscus, *H. syriacus*, a deciduous shrub with smaller flowers in softer shades of pink, blue, white and mauve. It has only become widely known in the last few years that there are native hibiscus, many of them valued by the Aboriginal as sources of food and fibres, which are attractive ornamental plants.

The yellow hibiscus, *H. panduriformis,* is a soft, woody shrub reaching about 2 metres. The yellow flowers may measure 9 centimetres across.

T here are about 300 species of *Hibiscus*, part of the family Malvaceae, and between 30 and 40 of these are found in Australia, usually in the tropical or sub-tropical areas, although one or two are native to Victoria. The short-lived flowers are generally large with 5 spreading petals uniting at the base to form a short tube from which a single column of fused stamen filaments surrounding the solitary style emerges. The pollen bearing anthers are arranged around the column below the projecting style with its branching 5-lobed stigma.

Many of the native hibiscus have yellow, white or soft pink flowers with a deep contrasting colour in the throat and although lasting for only one day are quickly replaced by fresh ones. The leaves vary in shape but are almost always covered with fine, star-shaped hairs and the pods, too, may contain small hairs which can cause skin troubles.

Edible beauties

Botanically speaking, the roots are not tuberous but in many species they are thick, fleshy, starch-filled and edible, either raw or cooked, as are the leaves, buds and young shoots. The bark provides long fibres which are water resistant and may be used for weaving into nets, dilly bags and so forth.

The bladder hibiscus or ketnia, *H. trionum*, is one of the few annual species, growing into a bushy plant 40–60 centimetres tall with coarsely-toothed leaves divided into 3–5 lobes and carrying, in summer, 7 centimetre creamy yellow flowers with brownish-red throats. As the fruiting pods mature, the calyces swell, giving the plant its common name. The bladder hibiscus, native to Africa and Asia as well as being widespread in Australia, is cultivated as a garden annual overseas but is regarded as a weed in Queensland, where it is very common, especially in the heavy, black soil areas.

The swamp or native hibiscus, *H. diversifolius*, is found from Sydney northwards through Queensland, generally flourishing along the banks of streams or other sites with a permanent water supply. It is a rather stiff, spreading, open bush, about 2 metres tall, the branches and leaf stalks covered with prickles. The leaves, edible when young, have roughly toothed margins and, while about 8 centimetres long, vary enormously in shape, being oblong, heart-shaped, circular or even with 3–5 lobes. The primrose yellow flowers, 4–5 centimetres long, with almost black throats, are carried in arching terminal sprays.

Variable flowers

The leaves of the native rosella or green kurrajong, *H. heterophyllus*, are almost twice the

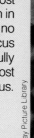

The Chinese hibiscus is the species most commonly seen in gardens, but it is by no means the only hibiscus that can be successfully grown, nor is it the most spectacular of the genus.

The bladder hibiscus is an annual hibiscus growing to about 60 centimetres in height. It has proven to be a good bedding plant and, in full sun and well composted soil, it puts on a spectacular summer display.

The native rosella *H. heteropyllus,* is a tall growing species reaching 6 metres. The young red buds (right) and new growth are edible, either cooked or raw. The opened flowers (below) are somewhat variable, ranging from soft pink to white. This is a hardy species under cultivation, favouring a sunny position and a temperate environment. It is not a difficult species to propagate, and may be grown from seeds or cuttings.

International Photo Library

size and just as diverse in shape as those of the swamp hibiscus. A native of the north-eastern regions of Australia, it prefers an open situation and plenty of moisture where it grows into a tall, upright, rather open shrub or even a small, 6 metre tree. The flowers, 10 centimetres across, may be pink or white, occasionally yellow, with a deep purple throat and the flowering time, usually summer, may begin in spring or extend into autumn. Like those of the Jamaica sorelle or rosella, *H. sabdariffa*, the fleshy calyces may be eaten raw or made into jelly; the young buds, roots and shoots are also edible. The pale, smooth wood is a good conductor of sound and is used for musical instruments. The inland rosella, *H. ficulneus*, also known as the native rosella, is reputed to cause dermatitis in horses, causing the hair to fall out, but the young pods, like those of the exotic, tropical okra, *H. esculentus*, are edible.

One of the native hibiscus which has been cultivated as an ornamental and used extensively as a street tree in Queensland, is the cotton tree or cottonwood, *H. tilaceus*. Growing naturally along the coast of Queensland and in many of the Pacific Islands, the cottonwood is a small tree, 7 metres tall, with a spreading head and light green foliage. The long-stalked, heart-shaped leaves, up to 12 centimetres across, are smooth, mid-green above but grey-white below. The black-eyed yellow flowers, about 14 centimetres across, appear in the leaf axils in spring and continue for months.

The roots, like those of many other species, were prized by the Aboriginals for food and the shoots, too, were eaten — but only in hard times, as they are as acid as sorrel leaves. The mucilaginous bark provided long fibres used in fishing nets and were also chewed to assuage thirst. The timber of cottonwood is attractively patterned and easily worked.

Spectacular blooms

The hollyhock tree or splendid hibiscus, *H. splendens*, is one of the largest-flowered species with blooms 12–18 centimetres in diameter. It flourishes along the coastal regions of northern

An excellent plant for gardens in the northern half of Australia, the yellow hibiscus responds well to pruning, although it may die back in winter.

ANT Tom & Pam Gardner

The cottonwood, *H. tilaceus* (right), is a coast lover, rarely being found far from the ocean. It is quite common in Queensland, and also occurs on many Pacific Islands, including Lord Howe.

ANT M. O'Connor

H. rhodopetalus is a tropical species, found in areas such as the Paluma Range near Townsville, Queensland. In terms of beauty, it is the equal of almost any other hibiscus species.

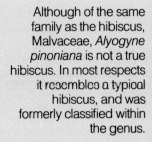

ANT B Thomson

Although of the same family as the hibiscus, Malvaceae, *Alyogyne pinoniana* is not a true hibiscus. In most respects it resembles a typical hibiscus, and was formerly classified within the genus.

ANT I.R. McCann

H. goldsworthii is a medium-sized Western Australian with prickly hairs on its stems and foliage. It is found only in the north-west of the State, favouring continually warm conditions and full sun.

An erect shrub growing to 2 metres, *H. divaricatus* is confined to northern Western Australia and the Northern Territory. It is fairly tolerant under cultivation, unless given an excessively damp soil.

Alyogyne hakeifolia (below) is another species bearing great resemblance to the hibiscus. An open shrub from South Australia and Western Australia, it does very well in cultivation except when subjected to harsh frosts.

A. Fox Auscape Int.

ANT I.R. McCann

New South Wales and Queensland in sandy, well-drained soils, growing into a large, bushy shrub 2–3 metres or even 4 metres tall with velvety, silver-grey foliage. The 15 centimetre leaves are heart-shaped or, sometimes, lobed, while the branches are thorny. The long-stalked flowers, carried in the leaf axils, are variable in colour but most are pink with deep red throats.

Not all hibiscus grow in the well-watered eastern States; a number grow in the drier areas of central Australia, mostly smaller shrubs, and some are found in the inland regions of Western Australia. The yellow hibiscus, *H. panduriformis*, is a small shrub, 1–2 metres tall, with long-stalked, woolly leaves, up to 10 centimetres across, sometimes divided into three lobes with the margins cut into rounded teeth. The flowers, 3–10 centimetres in diameter, are bright yellow or greenish-yellow with deep red throats. It grows on the banks of streams in the north of Western Australia and eastwards into the Northern Territory, and is also found in Asia and Africa.

Other Western Australians include the upright *H. divaricatus* with prickly 2 metre stems, lance-shaped leaves and, in spring, 10 centimetre bright yellow flowers, and *H. goldsworthii* whose lilac-coloured blooms have red eyes and whose foliage is covered in fine sharp hairs which attach themselves to any touching surface.

Close relatives

The sand hibiscus and the knobby hibiscus, despite their common names, are not true hibiscus but belong to closely related genera. The sand hibiscus, *Alyogyne pinoniana*, is a shrub, 1–3 metres tall, with variable but often palmately-lobed leaves, heavily veined on the lower surface. Leaves and stems are coated with fine hairs. The flowers, 4–6 centimetres long, are lilac-coloured with deep-red centres and are carried in the leaf axils near the ends of the branches, opening from late winter to early summer.

The sand hibiscus differs from *Hibiscus* species in botanical details, including the shape of the style which is not divided at the tip. It is found in the sandy stretches of the north-west coast and in the deserts of the Northern Territory and South Australia.

The knobby hibiscus, *Radyera farragei*, also has an undivided style but the seed capsule is divided into 10, not 5 compartments as in *Alyogyne*. It is a 1–3 metre shrub, growing on the edge of the arid interior of Western Australia where the rainfall is low and uncertain. The velvety green leaves are almost circular, green above and felted white below. The rosy-purple, dark-eyed flowers are carried in small axillary or terminal clusters in late spring. ●

EUCALYPTS

Australia's most ubiquitous tree

Bay Picture Library

The tenacious gum tree can be seen in nearly every type of habitat, from the tip of north Australia to the southern reaches of Tasmania, except for the most arid region of desert and the deepest rainforest. There are approximately 700 species in the genus *Eucalyptus*, about 95 per cent of which are found in Australia. The other five per cent grow in the southern Philippines, southern New Guinea and the Mollucas.

Australia is envied for its gum trees as they are thought to have more commercial uses than any other tree in the world. As a fast-growing hardwood they are used in the timber industry, particularly the jarrah and karri trees and the river red gum, *Eucalyptus camaldulensis*. Also eucalypt oil is used for pharmaceuticals and perfumed products. In Chile, Brazil and Argentina, the tree is grown extensively simply as a means of producing oil.

The eucalypt is also cultivated widely throughout the world for the reclamation of land as it grows well on difficult and seemingly poor soil. All it needs is moisture and a few minerals.

In addition to these uses, the eucalypt tree produces blossoms which attract the honey bee, its leaves provide medicinal eucalyptus oil and from the timber, tannin is extracted.

The beautiful red-flowering gum, *Eucalyptus ficifolia*, is a native of Western Australia. It grows best in heavy soils. The flowers may be pink or orange.

The river red gum, *Eucalyptus camaldulensis*, is found beside rivers throughout the mainland states. Its robust trunk can withstand flooding and its branches spread widely. It is one of the grandest and most imposing of the eucalypts.

Tall and decorative

However, it is as a decorative tree that the gum is most prized and loved. The variety of form, the colours of the trunks, their enormous height and the variety of flowers have been celebrated by artists and poets since the settlement of the continent. The *Eucalyptus regnans* of Victoria and Tasmania, which often grows to 100 metres, is the second tallest flowering plant in the world, exceeded only by the Californian redwood.

The name eucalyptus was first given to the plant by a French botanist, L'Heritier, who studied the plants brought back by French explorers who visited Tasmania in the eighteenth century. The name itself comes from the Greek words 'eu' meaning well and 'kalyptos' meaning covered, referring to the cap which covers the flower bud. The cap is distinctive of the genus and forms the nutty cradle which is depicted in the 'Bib and Bub', 'Snuggle Pot' and 'Cuddle Pie' fiction folklore. Its form, however, varies as regards the fusion or non-fusion of petals and sepals.

Suited to Mediterranean countries

Since Australia's earliest settlement, the seeds have been exported to Europe and have grown particularly well in Mediterranean climates. The *Eucalyptus citriodora* in particular has now become a distinctive, almost naturalised, part of the landscape in the South of France, Italy, California, Greece, South Africa, and throughout North Africa and China.

Victorian botanist, Sir Ferdinand von Mueller was one of the pioneers of its seed distribution throughout the world during his term from 1856 to 1873 as Director of the Melbourne Botanic Gardens. His exportation of the eucalypt to Italy facilitated the draining of the Pontine marshes in Lombardy which had been responsible for widespread malaria. Von Mueller also raised thousands of seedlings at the Botanical Gardens for distribution along the streets of towns throughout Victoria.

The Adelaide Botanic Gardens grew the first scientific stand of eucalyptus species in the 1860s and since that time they have been given a special niche in all state botanic gardens.

Decorative in gardens

As a decorative species, eucalypts were used by the Victorian landscape designer Edna Walling in many important gardens in and around Melbourne. In her book on street planting, *The Open Road*, published in the 1930s, she applauded their use throughout the urban, suburban and country environments. Since then, no domestic garden has seemed complete without its eucalyptus tree and, with so many

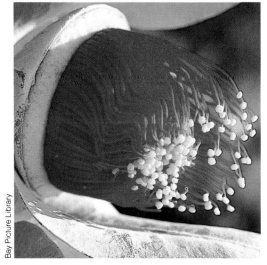

The most spectacular feature of this small twisted tree, *Eucalyptus macrocarpa*, is its flowers which untuck from their cap with each fine red filament topped by a bobbly yellow anther.

The *Eucalyptus caesia* has a beautiful flower and a weeping habit which has been developed in its cultivar, 'Silver Princess'. Its ghostly white hanging branches are most ornamental viewed over the fences and walls of gardens.

The flowers of the fuchsia gum, *Eucalyptus forrestiana*, a native of Western Australia, bear a striking resemblance to the plant of the same common name, with its drooping flower head.

71

species to choose from, there is a suitable species for every spot.

The most famous and perhaps the most beautiful flowering gum is the *Eucalyptus ficifolia*. Usually a small tree in domestic gardens, it can grow up to 14 metres when grown under irrigation and its crown of brilliant red flowers in summer is one of the most spectacular floral sights, particularly in its native Western Australia. The tree seems less happy in the eastern states but can be grown successfully.

The *Eucalyptus macrocarpa* is also from Western Australia. It is a small bent tree with large, beautiful pink to crimson flowers, a large 'cap' and brilliantly contrasting silver foliage. Another superb flowering gum from Western Australia is the *Eucalyptus caesia* which has a weeping habit. It has silver leaves and pink blossoms which hang down. This tree can also be grown in the eastern states but usually with difficulty. A recognised cultivar, *Eucalyptus caesia* 'Silver Princess' is easier to grow. The *Eucalyptus forrestiana* with its golden anthers and and the *Eucalyptus sideroxylon*, the pink flowering ironbark, are easier subjects for eastern gardens.

Any size or shape

It is possible to get a eucalypt of almost any size and shape to fit in with a domestic garden. Trees of the weeping habit are the *Eucalyptus nicholii*, the willow-leafed peppermint, the *Eucalyptus desmondendis* from Western Australia and the elegant, smooth-barked *Eucalyptus scoparia*. Those trees of grand, upright proportions are the *Eucalyptus grandis*, the flooded gums, which grow naturally in the forests of southern Queensland and have immense, straight, thick trunks and glossy crowns of leaves or the *Eucalyptus diversicolor*, the karris, which grow to great heights in the forests of Western Australia.

As salt-resistant wind breaks, gum trees are superb. One of the most useful and attractive trees for coastal and semi-coastal locations is the *Eucalyptus botryoides*, the mahogany gum. Its bushy crown can be heavily pruned and it is extremely fast-growing. It has white flowers which form star-like clusters and it is widespread on the coast and on the mountains and tablelands. It favours rich soil and, besides being a good tree for streets and parks, it is useful as a source of food for koalas.

The famous River Red Gum

A gum tree for growing on lawns or in large spaces is the magnificent river red gum, *Eucalyptus camaldulensis*, which can be grown in all mainland states. In its natural state it forms superb forests of immense height growing up

The red ironbark, *Eucalyptus sideroxylon*, has a narrow, straightish trunk wih a deeply-furrowed bark which is almost black and it bears cream, pink or red flowers.

The *Eucalyptus scoparia* is found only in a very restricted area of the Queensland/New South Wales border near Wallangarra.

The flooded gum, *Eucalyptus grandis*, is a fast-growing tree with a smooth white bark. It has some resistance to frost and is thriving as far south as Canberra Botanic Gardens.

The karri, *Eucalyptus diversicolor*, is a tall, straight tree which forms magnificent forests in the south west corner of Western Australia, where it is highly-prized for its timber.

C.A. Henley Auscape Int.

The true snow gum was originally known as *Eucalyptus niphophila* but its name is now considered a sub-species of *Eucalyptus pauciflora*.

The decorative flowers and leaves of *Eucalyptus kruseana*, together with its smooth red bark, make this gum tree a favourite for many gardeners.

Bay Picture Library

to 40 metres. It is one of the original trees on the site of the Royal Melbourne Botanic Gardens. One in particular of these trees is the 'Separation Tree' under which the citizens of Melbourne gathered in 1853 to hear the proclamation of State separation between Victoria and New South Wales. A river red gum also marks the spot in the Menindee National Park in northern New South Wales from which the explorers Burke, Wills and King set off on the fateful trip to Cooper's Creek with a retinue of camels.

Stands of gum trees

The eucalyptus forests of Australia are slowly being felled for timber on a scientific management basis. Many artificial forests have been planted using the *Eucalyptus nitens*, the shining gum, which is particularly fast-growing and prized by the wood pulp industry throughout Tasmania and Victoria.

Some impressive stands of naturally-occurring eucalypts are in the forests of the Dandenongs, the Upper Yarra regions and around Cumberland Falls where high rainfalls produce trees of immense height and girth. However, most experts agree that the karri forests of Western Australia are the most spectacular of all the eucalypt forests. Also the *Eucalyptus citriodora* forms forests on the north coast of Queensland and the tablelands. It has a marvellous white trunk and twisting upper branches. Its leaves are bright green and it exudes a superb lemon scent which makes it a popular domestic tree.

Hardy survivors

The most endearing quality of the eucalypt seems to be its ability to endure the onslaughts of nature. Trees ravaged by bushfires with blackened trunks are generally green with new growth one year later. They have the ability to regenerate even in the poorest of soils. Strangely enough, fire is often necessary to germinate the seeds which are encased in a tough capsule. After a fire it is not unusual to find the ground around a tree bright with seedlings.

One of the most amazing forms of the eucalypt is the mallee which takes its name from its habit of forming a multiple of stems directly, or almost directly, from out of the ground. The lignotubers, which are bulbs at the base of the plant, store food and produce many thin trunks rather than a single robust trunk. This evolved from growing in the poor, sandplain country of the southwestern part of New South Wales, Victoria and South Australia.

The forests of these trees formed almost impenetrable thickets for early pioneers who cleared as much of the land as they could, leaving the lignotubers in the ground. These later became a source of firewood.

Equally remarkable are the snow gums, *Eucalyptus pauciflora* of the Snowy Mountains region of New South Wales which can withstand freezing conditions. Their striped trunks and spreading form look stunning against a landscape of glaring snow.

Variable leaf forms

Often eucalyptus trees are hard to definitely identify as their leaves change as the tree goes from the juvenile to adult form. In some species, the tree retains a mixture of the two forms and in others the juvenile form is retained for the whole of the plant's life.

These species are often grown specifically for the beauty of their white and silver foliage. A selection of these are the *Eucalyptus kruseana*, *Eucalyptus pulverulenta* and *Eucalyptus crucis*.

FERNS

A *potted edition*

A.N.T. Joselyr Burt

The fern is one of the oldest members of the botanical world and to have your potted fern simply filling an otherwise bare corner, is doing this senior citizen of the plant world an injustice.

Ferns are among the oldest members of the botanical world, predating flowering plants by some 200 million years. Fossil evidence indicates the existence of ferns in the Palaeozoic era, about 300 million years ago. They were among the earliest organisms to inhabit dry land and the first plants to develop roots and leaves as well as stems.

Along with the aquatic algae (psilopsids), horsetails (sphenopsids) and lycopsids (clubmosses), ferns (pteropsids) were the raw material of the earth's original coal seams.

Ferns went into a decline as the climate became drier and by the Mesozoic era about 135 million years ago flowering plants (angiosperms) and plants bearing naked seeds (gymnosperms) had become dominant and ferns were left to occupy remaining hospitable moist climes.

Some 335 species are native to Australia although hundreds of ferns now exist only in fossil form. These casts are all that remain as evidence of their dominance in ancient times.

Damp niches on a dry continent

In Australia ferns are found mainly on the east coast, especially areas with high rainfall. Their wide range of habitats includes tropical and subtropical rainforests, open eucalypt forest, watercourses, coastal headlands and inland plains. Their delicate appearance is belied by their hardiness and they even can be seen clinging to cliffs constantly exposed to sea spray, in sub-alpine clefts, on sandhills and in the gorges of central Australia.

Some ferns thrive in warm moist conditions with high humidity and temperature but some species, especially the tree ferns, do best in cooler surroundings.

This soft tree fern at Wilsons Promontory, Victoria is a protected species.

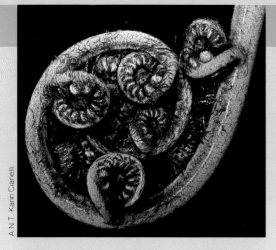

A Cooper's tree fern (left) unrolls a new leaf. All except one species of fern grow this way.

Common maidenhair fern, *Adiantum aethiopicum* (right), has short rhizomes and filmy leaves. The most delicate of the ferns favour rocky and moist situations.

The sori on the underside of a frond (left).

Five-fingered jack or rough maidenhair, *A. hispidulum* (right), is the most distinctive of the maidenhairs. It has long finger-like fronds with rectangular leaves; young fronds are pink.

Northern maidenhair, *A. cunninghamii* (right), is a tropical to sub-tropical Queensland species in rainforests from the coasts to the mountains. The new fronds of this fern are pink. Growing with this fern is the green prickly rasp fern, *Doodia aspera*.

What makes ferns distinct

Ferns and fern allies reproduce by spores. Modern plants, on the other hand, reproduce using flowers and seeds.

The lifecycle consists of two distinct stages known as an alternation of generations. Spores develop in a case called the sporangium, which is surrounded by a ring of cells and occur in lumpy groups (call sori) on the underside or edges of a frond. Once the spores are ripe the sporangium bursts open and the spores are scattered on the wind. Having landed, and given the damp conditions required for germination, a spore develops in a few weeks into a tiny heart-shaped leaf-like body called the prothallus (or gametophyte). This contains both male and female sexual organs and when the latter's egg cells are fertilised a new fern is born. This grows into a sporophyte or spore-bearing fern and the prothallus soon withers away and dies.

Some ferns do not rely on spores but reproduce vegetatively. In bird's nest ferns (Asplenium genus) and several others, small buds (bulbils) are formed on the fronds and eventually drop and take root in the ground. Bracken ferns, among the most widespread of the world's plants, have root-like branching stems (rhizomes) from which new plants are continually formed. ●

The pouched coral fern, *Gleichenia dicarpa* (right), is light green with numerous forked fronds. Distinctive are the pouch-like lobes along the edges. Commonly found growing on cliffs and in swampy areas.

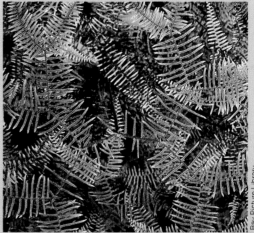

Cooper's tree fern, *Cyathea cooperi* (left).

Most would never expect to see a fern surrounded by snow but in the southern alps it is very common. The rough tree fern *C. australis* (right), is found in wet forests, gullies and on creek beds.

Elkhorns and staghorns belong to the *Platycerium* genus, and like the bird's nest fern are protected in northern rainforests. The staghorn, *P. superbum* (right), grows singly on tree trunks.

The elkhorn, *P. bifurcatum* (left), grows in clumps and like the staghorn is a popular wall-garden plant.

The king fern, *Angiopteris evecta* (left), is reputed to have the largest fronds of any fern and can grow to five metres. With age this fern develops a trunk.

Epiphyte ferns are ones that grow on other trees or rocks. The birds nest fern, *Asplenium australasicum* (right), has bright green fronds which grow to 100 centimetres.

The girstle fern, *Blechnum cartilagineum* (left).

Rock ferns, *Cheilanthes tenuifolia* (right) survive semi-arid and often shadless regions of the interior. These ferns are known as the resurrection plants because of their ability to regenerate after apparently withering away.

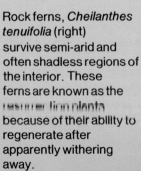

A.N.T. R & D Keller

Bay Picture Library

76

DECORATIVE DRYANDRAS

Western Australians of rare beauty

Western Australia is home to many beautiful plants, but few come close to matching the beauty of the dryandras. The showy dryandra is one of the most spectacular of the genus.

ANT J Bronwlie

Some of the most attractive among the strange and unusual wildflowers of Western Australia are the dryandras, *Dryandra*, prized not only for their flowers but also for their decorative foliage. The genus, which takes its name from the Swedish botanist, Jonas Dryander, is closely related to the *Banksia* and there are somewhere between 50 and 60 species, ranging in size from low-growing, prostrate shrubs to those which may reach 5 metres in height.

I n their natural state dryandras are found only in the south-west corner of Western Australia and some species are so particular in their requirements that they are confined to very limited areas of that region.

Flowers and foliage are both valued by florists for fresh and dried arrangements but for several reasons the plants, particularly some of the larger types, are not cultivated widely in the eastern States. Although seed germinates easily, young plants are prone to damping off — a fatal disease of seedlings. The plants require very specific growing conditions and the habit of growth of the bigger shrubs is often straggly, making them difficult to place in a suburban garden.

Root fungus

One of the major problems with the cultivation of dryandras is their susceptibility to the root fungus *Phytophthora cinnamomi*. This fungus, which attacks the roots' growth areas, is seldom solely responsible for the death of a plant, but by weakening the root system it leaves the plant vulnerable to a wide range of other diseases.

The signs of attack by this fungus are not usually noticed until it is too late. The plant will suddenly wilt and, within a few days it will die. Often, particularly with dryandras, wilting will occur soon after flowering, as at this time the plant is in a weakened state from having diverted all its energies to reproduction.

There is, unfortunately, no way of achieving satisfactory results against *P. cinnamomi* once it becomes established, but in the case of dryandras there are ways of preventing its emergence. One way is to spread a layer of limestone chips below the plant before planting. Studies so far carried out suggest that the fungus is inhibited by the presence of calcium in the soil.

Raised garden beds also provide some means

The showy dryandra (above) is a tall shrub with open branches reaching about 4 metres in height. In rocky locations, such as here on Bluff Knoll in the Stirling Ranges, it is often shorter and takes on a windswept shape. *Dryandra polycephala* (left) has performed better in east coast gardens than many other dryandra species, but it is still a difficult plant to grow. It reaches about 3 metres, flowering in spring and producing many large, bright yellow flowerheads.

Auscape International Esther Beaton

ANT R & D Kelt

Denise Greig

Dryandras flower at various times of the year, but late winter and spring are favoured. Many will flower continuously over several months.

D. nivea (right) is a low growing species that rarely surpasses 15 centimetres. The finely serrated leaves form an attractive part of the plant, and loosely surround the flowerheads.

Denise Greig

The cut leaf dryandra (right) is the species best suited to cultivation thus far; it does well in Canberra and Melbourne, and has been grafted onto *Banksia serrata* with success. If a well drained, partly shaded position, with an underlying bed of lime is provided, it usually grows quite freely. This species grows to about 2 metres, and bears bright yellow flowerheads in spring.

ANT I. McCann

of control, as *P. cinnamomi* requires free water to spread. Perfect drainage is also essential to grow many other natives, as there is a wide spectrum of plants that are susceptible to this fungus.

Trial grafting

Perhaps the most promising method of combating this fungus and successfully growing dryandras is to graft them onto resistant rootstock, such as banksia. However, it may be some time before such plants become widely available, as trials are still very much in the experimental stage.

In many respects the dryandras closely resemble banksia. Their leaves vary greatly in shape, but are generally stiff, lobed or sawtoothed, and often are prickly.

The flowers are most commonly yellow or orange although a few are red, pink or purple. The individual flowers — long, slender tubes divided at the mouth into 4 narrow segments — are crowded into dense heads surrounded at the base by persistent bracts. Unlike the long spikes of banksia flowers, the heads are, by and large, broadly cone-shaped. They may be terminal, at the ends of the stems, or lateral, arising from the leaf axils. Dryandra flowers produce large quantities of nectar, which makes them a favourite with honeyeaters.

Winged seeds

Each hair-covered, woody seed container, looking like a seed itself, holds two winged seeds which, in some species, are released on maturity but in others remain enclosed until the right conditions are present.

The showy dryandra, *Dryandra formosa*, is one of the rich variety of Western Australian native flowers seen on the Stirling Ranges and the stony hillsides around Albany. It is a large, open, rather brittle shrub, 2–4 metres tall, with soft leaves, 10–12 centimetres long but very narrow and deeply divided into triangular lobes. In winter and spring, glowing, deep yellow flowerheads, 10 centimetres across, with hundreds of sweetly scented flowers packed onto each cone-shaped base, are carried at the ends of the branches.

The parrot bush or holly-leaf dryandra, *D. sessilis* (syn. *D. floribunda*) grows freely over a much larger area stretching from Geraldton to Esperance. The rounded, pale yellow flowerheads, filled with nectar, appear in winter and spring, contrasting attractively with the dark green, holly like foliage cut into sharply pointed lobes.

The downy, mid-green leaves of the tangled honey-pot, *D. pteridifolia*, are three or four times as long as those of the showy dryandra as they sometimes reach 40 centimetres. When mature, they have long, narrow, widely spaced, pointed lobes and when young they are deep soft pink. The plant is prostrate, usually less than 50 centimetres tall and the creamy-yellow flowerheads, 6–7 centimetres across and tinged with pink, are held very close to the ground. Its native habitat is on sandy heathlands from the south coast north towards Lake Grace.

Flowers change colour

The pendulous flowers of *D. speciosa*, a straggling shrub growing to just over 1 metre, are silvery when in bud, salmon-pink when first open and brownish-yellow when mature. The leaves, unlike those of most of the dryandras, are not toothed.

While the yellow blooms of *D. polycephala* are smaller than those of many other species they are produced in great profusion each spring, along the slender branches of this upright shrub which may be 2–3 metres tall. The yellow-green leaves are long and very narrow with pointed, widely spaced lobes.

One of the dryandras which is sometimes available commercially in the eastern States, is the cut-leaf dryandra, *D. praemorsa*. It grows into a large, bushy shrub about 2.5 metres tall and almost as broad. The stiff, prickly leaves are cut short at the tip and the large yellow flowerheads, with their abundance of nectar, are conspicuous in spring.

There are many other species but few plants are seen outside their native State. Various methods of cultivation are being tested and perhaps in time these most attractive Western Australians will be met frequently in the east. ●

ANT I. McCann

Denise Greig

ANT A & S Tinga

D. carlinoides, the spiky dryandra, is a low growing shrub to about 1 metre. It is restricted to areas between Perth and Kalbarri in Western Australia where it grows on sandy plains and heaths. This specimen was photographed near Gin Gin.

The large yellow flowerheads of *D. quercifolia,* the oak-leaved dryandra, begin as orange buds. The mature flowerhead retains the orange as a soft tint on its edge. The flowers of this rounded shrub appear in autumn and winter.

The golden dryandra, *D. nobilis* (below), prefers the gravelly soils of woodlands in Western Australia's south-west. The flowerheads have a weeping appearance until they burst into full flower and become much fuller.

CLIMBING PLANTS

They make their way up in the world

The attractive coral vine, *Kennedia coccinea*.

ANT A&S Tingay

This spectacular hoya (right) is native to Cape York rainforests. The flowers may be up to 6 centimetres across.

The flame pea (below) has spectacular orange or red flowers and is a proficient twiner. Most species are endemic to Western Australia.

This species of clematis or traveller's joy (right) will often twist itself around supporting shrubs. Its creamy-white flowers appear in spring.

Most plants can support themselves as they grow towards the light which is essential to their continued development but some are too weak to stand erect. They must either crawl along the ground or find another plant to hold them upright. These plants are known as trailers, ground covers, ramblers and climbers.

The distinction between the groups is not always hard and fast, as conditions can alter their behaviour. Many vigorous trailers and ground covers, such as the dusky coral pea, *Kennedia rubicunda*, remain prostrate only if there are no trees or shrubs nearby, but they will climb 2–3 metres if given support. The stems of ramblers are often semi-erect when young but as they lengthen they arch over, building the plant into a dense thicket. If the stems carry thorns they are more easily caught and held by the branches of other bushes, sometimes engulfing them.

Wait-a-while has sharp spines

To help in their struggle to the sunlight, true climbers have developed definite means such as hooked thorns and prickles, aerial roots, tendrils or a twining growth pattern. The white flowered native raspberry, *Rubus hillii*, with its edible red fruits, is a scrambling shrub with sharp, short prickles on both leaves and stems. A group of palms known as the lawyer canes or wait-a-whiles, *Calamus* species, are true climbers of the rainforests, rising many metres by means of needle-like spines and sturdy hooks on stems, leaves and flower stalks. In spite of this armament, the stems of the lawyer canes are harvested for making cane furniture.

Aerial roots grow from nodes along the stems, clinging tightly to any roughened surface such as tree trunks and rock faces. This method of climbing is common to many rainforest plants including some which are now cultivated indoors. These include *Rhaphiodophora australasica*, with glossy elliptical leaves up to 40 centimetres long; the early stages of native peppers, *Piper* species — tall climbers closely related to the commercial peppers of Malaysia — and *Pothos longipes* which has been known to reach 15 metres in length as its aerial roots carry it up trunks and over mossy rocks. The leaves of this *Pathos* are most distinctive and unusual as the narrow leaf blade is carried on a longer, flattened leaf-like stalk up to 15 centimetres long. The minute flowers are closely packed into a thick spike and are followed by small, oval, edible red fruits.

ANT R. & D. Keller

ANT G. Cheers

The pepper vine (far left), seen mostly in tropical regions, is a useful root climber for shaded gardens and can be cultivated as an indoor plant. The wonga vine (left) is a strong climber. Its attractive tubular flowers appear in spring.

ANT I.R. McCann

The *Glycine camescens* (above) is a stem twister which attaches itself to other plants. Its pea-like flowers occur most of the year.

A wonga vine (left) twined around a *Banksia marginata*. The vine's glossy, pinnate leaves grow to 7 centimetres.

Bay Picture Library

Traveller's joy or old man's beard

Many climbers use twining shoots, or tendrils, twisting them around any possible support. These tendrils, which are modified leaves or shoots, are thread-like and supple when young but become rigid once curled about their host. Well-known as an indoor plant and ground cover, the native grape or kangaroo vine, *Cissus antarctica*, from Queensland and New South Wales, and *C. hypoglauca*, whose habitat also stretches into Victoria, are both vigorous climbers using tendrils to carry them aloft. The soft curling shoots grow from the stem opposite the base of the leaf stalk. While both have small flowers and blue-black fruit, they are easily distinguished as the native grape has solitary, toothed leaves while *C. hypoglauca* has five-stalked leaflets radiating from the tip of the main leaf stalk.

In some climbers the leaf stalk takes over the job of the tendrils. By this means traveller's joy or old man's beard, *Clematis aristata*, extends in tangled masses among the tops of trees and shrubs in all the eastern states. Its springtime canopy of starry, creamy-white flowers is followed by a delicate blanket of 1-seeded fruits bearing long, plumed tails of silvery-white silky hairs. Four other clematis are native to Australia; one, *C. gentianoides*, found only in Tasmania, is not a climber but a small suckering shrub. The others are all vigorous climbers similar to old man's beard. *C. glycinoides*, is a native of Queensland, New South Wales and Victoria and has

The dusky coral pea (right) will climb 2–3 metres if given support of trees or shrubs. The Rosea or Bower of Beauty (far right) is a strong twiner which bears large, pink, trumpet-shaped flowers.

Bay Picture Library

The hardy clematis (above) is ideal for covering fences in sun or semi-shade. White flowers appear in spring followed by feathery fruits. The purple coral pea (right) is a trailing plant which is used for ground cover in areas with well-drained soil.

glossier, smooth-edged leaves, while *C. microphylla*, which prefers drier conditions, is found in all states except the Northern Territory, and *C. pubescens* is a Western Australian native.

Clockwise climbers

The last and biggest group of climbers is composed of those which simply twine their flexible young stems around their hosts, in the southern hemisphere in a clockwise direction but in the northern half of the world in an anti-clockwise one. Climbers which use this method vary enormously in size.

Rampant vines climb from the dim forest floor up tall tree trunks to the bright light above, sometimes stretching for many metres from tree to tree and hanging in loops and swags. In some the stems reach 30 centimetres in diameter. Two of these powerful climbers or lianas, belong to the pea family. *Mucuna gigantea*, found in the Northern Territory, Queensland and New South Wales, has long, narrow leaflets carried in threes and big green flowers packed into pendant sprays 25–30 centimetres in length. The flat brown pods which follow are winged and covered in fine stinging hairs. The seeds were eaten by the explorer Ludwig Leichhardt who found that, after pounding and boiling, they made an acceptable substitute porridge but not coffee.

Native wisteria, *Milletia megasperma*, is just as vigorous as its exotic namesake. It has dark green leaves, bearing up to thirteen pointed leaflets,

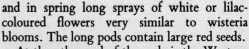

The lawyer vine (left) known as 'vicious hairy Mary' needs surrounding trees to climb. It is equipped with sharp spines and prefers shade.

and in spring long sprays of white or lilac-coloured flowers very similar to wisteria blooms. The long pods contain large red seeds.

At the other end of the scale is the Western Australian climbing sundew, *Drosera macrantha*, whose slender twining stem carries aloft delicate, pink or white 5-petalled flowers and glistening, sticky, insect-trapping leaves.

Climbers belong to many different families. Some of the most brightly coloured with butterfly-like blooms, such as the coral peas, *Kennedia* species, the false sasparilla, *Hardenbergia comptoniana*, and the vermillion flowered *Chorizema diversifolium* from Western Australia belong to Papilionaceae, once a sub-family of Leguminoseae, the pea family.

Although many of the largest and most vigorous climbers are found in the rainforests, they also thrive in more open and drier habitats. A few, like *Glycine canescens*, tolerate hard conditions and are at home in the dry watercourses or stoney soils of the arid inland.

Even ferns climb

Where logging has opened up swampy forest land climbing ferns thrive. The climbing swamp fern, *Stenochlaena palustris*, has long-creeping rhizomes which scramble and climb over bushes and up trees. The fronds are pinnate, the sterile ones with toothed margins, the fertile ones smooth. The climbing maidenhair, *Lygodium microphyllum* (syn. *L. scandens*), is the most widespread of this group of climbing ferns and has been known to reach 25m in length. It climbs not with the rhizome or stem but with the rhachis, the central axis of the frond. It continues to extend producing side branches and small fronds as it grows.

The wax flower (above) is a twining, aerial root climber native to Queensland's rainforests. The burny bean vine (left) is a twining climber which bears long, pendant sprays of green pea-flowers.

Welcome or unwelcome in gardens

An increasing number of Australian climbers are being cultivated as appreciation of their beauty and hardiness in the right positions spreads. These include the wonga-wonga vine, *Pandorea pandorana*, the pink-flowered bower of beauty, *P. jasminoides* 'Rosea', and some of the less well-known *Hoyas*.

However one group which is not welcome in any garden is the parasitic devil's guts or dodder-laurels, *Cassytha* species, of which there are about a dozen widespread across Australia. They germinate from seed, pushing roots into the ground, but soon become entirely dependent upon their hosts, twining through the branches of trees and shrubs in inextricable tangles. The leaves are reduced to tiny scales and the thread-like stems attach themselves by means of suckers through which they draw water and nutriment from the host. The little white or greenish flowers are either in small sprays or clusters, the rounded fruit which follow is usually green, black or orange-red. ●

IRISES

Short-lived charmers

Bay Picture Library

Like so many of the plants cultivated in Australian gardens, the many coloured bearded iris are not part of the native flora. There are, in fact, no indigenous *Iris* but there are other members of the Iris family, *Iridaceae*, usually called irises or flags, whose short-lived flowers, although not as large and spectacular as the exotic species, add colour and charm to the bush.

Flowers of the native irises last only a few hours, but they are quickly replaced by succeeding flowers.

The largest iris flowers are produced by *P. sericea,* a plant distinguished by its hairy appearance; the leaves and stems are covered by soft downy hairs.

Auscape Int. F. Ingwersen

These plants are all herbaceous with under ground storage systems, such as corms, tubers or rhizomes, grass-like foliage and flowers whose parts are arranged in threes, the calyx–sepals and corolla–petals combined into a coloured perianth with six segments. The seeds are carried in three-celled capsules which are usually triangular in cross-section. There are six Australian genera in the Iris family with about 30 species between them.

The largest group, the native iris or flags, *Patersonia*, contains about 20 indigenous species as well as a few which grow in south-east Asia. Their name does not commemorate 'Banjo' Paterson, the author of *Waltzing Matilda*, but a Scot, Colonel W. Paterson, who travelled extensively in South Africa during the eighteenth century. Generally the native iris form clumps of long, thin, grass-like foliage and the flowering stems carry terminal clusters of flowers enclosed in two boat-shaped bracts from which they emerge in succession, most commonly one at a time but in a few species two together. Each flower is short-lived, often lasting for less than one day.

With the exception of the Western Australian *P. xanthina*, whose blooms are yellow, the flowers of the native iris are in shades of blue or purple, contrasting with the yellow anthers in the centre. The three outer segments are large, broad and spreading, the three inner ones, small, upright and inconspicuous. The seed capsule is

Coastal sandstone areas are home to *P. glabrata*. It is a fairly common species, and perhaps the best known of the flag irises.

P. xanthia (below), a common species in the jarrah forests of Western Australia, is the only species to have yellow flowers.

Bay Picture Library

Bay Picture Library

long and narrow, splitting to release the mature brown seeds.

One of the most well known species in the eastern States, the native iris or leafy purple flag, *P. glabrata*, is often seen on the infertile coastal sandstones of eastern Queensland, New South Wales and Victoria. Unlike those of most other species the dark green leaves, 15–30 centimetres long, do not spring from the roots but clasp the bases of the flower stems. The blue or purple-blue flowers open in spring and measure 2–4 centimetres across.

Largest flowers

The showy, deep violet flowers of the silky purple flag, *P. sericea*, are the biggest of all the species. Carried on 30 centimetre stems in spring they often open in pairs. The foliage is dark, rather grey-green and the edges of the lower leaves, the flower stems and the dark bracts are covered with fine, silky, deciduous hairs, which give the plant its common name. The silky, purple flag is found in coastal areas of Queensland and New South Wales and occasionally in eastern Victoria, including the subalpine region.

The dwarf purple flag, *P. longifolia*, is similar to the silky purple flag but much smaller, the flower stems being only 15 centimetres tall. Its range is more restricted and does not extend into Queensland.

As the names imply the short purple flag, *P. fragilis*, carries its mauve flowers on stems shorter than the soft, rush-like leaves, which may be as long as 45 centimetres, while the long purple flag, *P. longiscapa*, has flower stalks up to 40 centimetres in length, holding the blue to purple blooms above the dense clumps of flat leaves.

Bright yellow flowers

The Western Australian species, as is the case with so many of their native plants, are not found in the eastern States. The yellow flag, *P. xanthina*, is common in the jarrah forests from Perth south to the coast. The bright yellow blooms, 3–4 centimetres across, are carried on long flower stems, 70 centimetres tall. Other flags growing in the south-west of the State include the hairy flag, *P. rudis*, with deep purple flowers, the enclosing bracts covered with long hairs, and the purple flag, *P. occidentalis*, the most widespread species, with 40 centimetre long leaves and mauve flowers 4–5 centimetres across. All these flags flower in the spring.

The morning iris, *Orthrosanthus* — orthro, morning and anthos, flower — takes both its common and botanical names from the way its flowers open early in the morning but fade quickly as the day becomes hot. There are 5 endemic species of morning iris with delicate blue, rarely white, flowers borne on branching stems in terminal clusters protected by papery bracts. Each bloom is about 2.5 centimetres across with

ANT I. McCann

P. longifolia (left) reaches about 50 centimetres in height, with a flower stem as long or longer than the leaves.

P. fragilis (below), unlike many other species, will tolerate damp conditions, and may be seen in open, poorly drained heathlands.

ANT Jutta Höse

6 equal segments spreading from a short, thin tube.

Like those of the native iris, the flowers of the morning iris open in succession and bloom through the spring months. *Orthrosanthus multiflorus* is found in sandy areas on the south coast of Victoria and South Australia while *O. laxus* grows in the south-west of Western Australia.

Morning iris

The starry white flowers of the grass flags, *Libertia*, are much smaller than those of the morning iris and are carried in larger, open branching clusters above fans of dark green foliage. The flowers have six, spreading, almost equal segments and the seed capsules are rounded. There are only 2 species, the pretty grass-flag, *L. pulchella*, flowering in spring and summer and growing in the cool, damp, mountain regions of Tasmania, Victoria and New South Wales and the larger-branching, grass-flag, *L. paniculata*, whose light green, 60 centimetre tussocks of foliage and bigger sprays of flowers may be seen in sandy woodland from the east coast of Victoria up to Brisbane.

The butterfly flag or white flag-iris, *Diplarrena moroea*, is very common along the south coast of New South Wales, in east Victoria and in Tasmania where it flourishes in a variety of conditions. In some places the tussocks of flat, green leaves, up to 60 centimetres tall, cover the ground between the trees and in the dappled light of spring and summer the flowers, on their long stems, flutter like butterflies about the foliage. The flower stalks are upright and carry 2–6 sweetly scented blooms protected in the bud by long, narrow bracts.

Like the native iris the butterfly iris opens its flowers in succession, each one composed of 3 large, rounded white segments and 3 smaller, inner ones which may be marked in yellow or mauve. The whole bloom is about 6 centimetres in diameter.

The only other species, the mountain flag, *D. latifolia*, is not so common being confined to the mountains of Tasmania. It is a larger and coarser plant and the flowers are more heavily marked with mauve or yellow.

Two other small genera belonging to the Iris family are also restricted to Tasmania. *Isophysis tasmanica* belongs to the wet mountain regions of the west and south-west of the island. The 15 centimetre tall foliage is similar to that of the cultivated bearded iris but the solitary flowers, up to 8 centimetres across on upright stalks, have six long, narrow, pointed, radiating segments, either dark reddish-purple or yellow. It flowers in summer. *Campynema lineare* is a small plant with a 30 centimetre stem bearing tiny, mustard yellow flowers with red anthers. It blooms in summer and autumn, growing on the mountains and badly drained button-grass plains. ●

The butterfly flag, *D. moroea* (above), is a showy species found along the east coast from Tasmania up to southern New South Wales.

L. paniculata is a tufted perennial that bears its attractive flowers in spring.

I. tasmanica is found only in the wet mountains of western and south-western Tasmania. Its unusual flowers may measure up to 8 centimetres across.

RICE-FLOWERS

Fast-growing, subtle beauties

The Qualup bell is one of the most attractive rice-flowers, but unfortunately is rarely seen in cultivation.

Jean-Paul Ferrero Auscape Int.

The yellow rice-flower grows in cool, moist areas of south-east Australia, particularly favouring forests and heathlands. Male and female bushes are readily distinguished, the female being decidedly less conspicuous than the male.

The smooth rice-flower occurs naturally in dry, hilly areas. Duplication of these conditions in cultivation, with well-drained, raised garden beds, will see it thrive. It reaches only about 30–50 centimetres, and is suited to rockery planting. The white flowers appear in spring and summer.

The rose banjine is another ideal rockery plant, often seen in cultivation in the eastern States; in Western Australia it is found in the jarrah forests. The leaves of this species are lanceolate in shape, and hooked at the ends, and as such differ from most other *Pimeleas*.

A rather difficult plant to grow in cultivation, the silky yellow banjine is one of the more dainty *Pimeleas*. Propagation, as with most other *Pimeleas*, is by cutting, and the plants must have partial shade and a well-drained bed.

These small relatives of the daphne may lack the size and grandeur of other native plants, but they make up for this with their own brand of subtle beauty. Their flowers are very attractive, and a welcome sight in the bush. Many have adapted well to cultivation, and are certainly worth a place in most gardens.

Apart from the few which grow in the tropics, most of the 80 or so species of *Pimelea* are shrubby plants, commonly no more than 1 metre in height. They are evergreens, dull evergreens.

In the eastern States they are known as rice-flowers, because of the rice-like appearance of those with white flowerheads, and in the west as banjines, from their Aboriginal name which refers to the strength of their fibrous bark. Most of them are endemic to Australia but some grow in New Zealand, New Guinea and other northern islands. Their botanical name, deriving from the Greek, *pimele*, 'fat', refers to the oiliness of the small seeds.

Form and colour

The leaves of rice-flowers are generally small and may be arranged in pairs or alternately. The flowers, some of them perfumed, are rather like daphne flowers, with long, narrow tubes, most often partly covered with silky hairs, ending in four spreading lobes. The normal number of projecting stamens is two but occasionally there is only one.

Colours include white, cream, yellow, pink and red. In some species the stalkless flowers are spread along the stems in small axillary clusters, but in the others are in rounded terminal heads subtended by four, or more, leaf-like bracts.

The most eye-catching of the *Pimeleas* and one not typical of the genus, is the Western Australian Qualup bell, *P. physodes*, which grows on sandy heathland and stoney hills south of Ravensthorpe. It takes its common name from an old homestead in the area. The Qualup bell is a sparse, upright shrub, well under 1 metre in height, with small oval leaves tidily arranged along the stems. The terminal clusters of numerous, small flowers, appearing in late winter and spring, are almost completely enclosed by the large, 3–5 centimetre long, cream, green and red bracts so that the whole flowerhead is drooping and bell-like. These bracts deepen in colour as they age. The Qualup bell is, unfortunately, among those *Pimeleas* most difficult to cultivate.

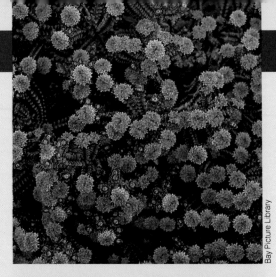

Nodding flowerheads

A yellow flowered Western Australian species, the silky yellow banjine, *P. suaveolens*, has nodding flowerheads 3–4 centimetres across. This is a variable species, but the flower tubes and lobes are usually long and very narrow while the yellow bracts are covered with hairs. It is generally a light, open shrub, less than 1 metre tall, with long, narrow leaves crowded together on the stems.

The pink rice-flower, *P. ferruginea* (syn *P. decussata*), although originating in Western Australia, is well-known as a cultivated plant in the eastern States. A compact shrub, about 1 metre tall and across, it has small, glossy green leaves in two pairs of neatly ordered rows. In spring the whole bush is covered with rounded heads of pink flowers.

Growing in the jarrah forests of Western Australia is another pink-flowered *Pimelea*, the rose banjine, *P. rosea*. Often smaller than the pink rice-flower, it has soft, narrow leaves, 1–2 centimetres long and, in spring, spreading, hairy rose-pink flowerheads, 2.25 centimetres across. A white flowered form of this banjine is now regarded as a separate species.

The banjine, *P. clavata*, is one of several species known as bootlace bushes as the tough bark can be stripped from the branches and used immediately like string, for lacing, tying or netting. The banjine is a tall Western Australian species growing into an open, upright shrub as much as 2.5 metres tall. The narrow leaves are about 4 centimetres long, and the small terminal clusters of spring and summer flowers are white.

Eastern species

Eastern bootlace bushes include *P. axiflora*, also known as the tough rice-flower. Another tall species, sometimes reaching 3–4 metres, it has long arching branches lightly clad with pairs of smooth narrow leaves up to 7 centimetres long and with clusters of creamy-white flowers in the axils. It is a forest shrub, at home in damp gullies.

Similar bark is found on the tall rice-flower, *P. ligustrina*, one of the most attractive of the eastern species and widespread from Queensland around to South Australia and in Tasmania, where it varies in size from a large rounded shrub to a small tree. The thin, ovate leaves are 5–7 centimetres long and, in summer, the foliage is almost covered by large white flowerheads with conspicuous, projecting stamens and backed by 4–6 large, reddish bracts.

Yet another white-flowered species, the slender rice-flower, *P. linifolia*, is very common in all the eastern States, usually in open or lightly timbered country. Its habit, leaves and flowers are all variable but it is usually a slender shrub under 1 metre tall. The leaves, about 2.5 centimetres long, may be linear to ovate. The flowerheads

An excellent feature plant, the pink rice-flower reaches about 1 metre in height and width, and bears masses of pink flowers in spring. Its shape is invariably neat and rounded. Although a native of Western Australia, it is quite common in the eastern States — hardly surprising considering its desirable qualities.

The tough rice-flower, *P. axiflora,* is a tall-growing species reaching 3–4 metres. Its beauty is quite subtle, as it does not produce the massed displays of its better known relatives. The long leaves, up to 7 centimetres in length, tend to dominate the bush and obscure the small flowers.

The tall rice-flower generally reaches about 2 metres in height, but is somewhat variable. It is extremely tolerant of shaded positions, and will attractively fill a seemingly 'unfillable' position. A variety of this species, *P. ligustrina* var. *hypericina* is now fairly common in cultivation, but has smaller flowers.

One of the most common rice-flowers, the slender rice-flower is found in all States except Western Australia. Two forms exist — that in the photograph and a suckering form found at the Botanic Gardens, Canberra. The latter shows great promise for cultivation.

One of the most attractive sights in alpine areas in summer is the alpine rice-flower, bursting forth in a profusion of pink or cream, scented flowers.

The downy rice-flower is a widespread species, most common in western Victoria. The reason for its name is quite obvious — the soft yellow flowers, and the leaves, are covered in fine hairs.

P. spectabilis is noted for its large flowerheads — the largest of the genus. Although not cultivated widely in the eastern States, it seems to perform well in Perth, given partial shade and well-drained soil.

are sometimes erect but may be nodding: in either case they are backed by four wide, smooth bracts, often tinged with red. The slender rice-flower, also known as the nodding rice-flower or button, is one of the small number of rice-flowers which are suspected of being poisonous to stock.

Low-growing species

Also in this group is the smooth rice-flower, *P. glauca*, a low-growing species found from South Australia through to Queensland, and in Tas-

mania where it makes a compact bush about 30 centimetres across and up to 50 centimetres in height. In spring and summer it carries terminal clusters of creamy-white flowers whose tubes are covered with white hairs.

Several other low-growing rice-flowers are found in the alpine and sub-alpine regions of New South Wales, Victoria and Tasmania, including short forms of the bootlace bushes, *P. axiflora* and *P. ligustrina*. The flowerheads of the latter with their large, crimson-tinged bracts, are among the most outstanding flowers in the region.

In summer the alpine rice-flower, *P. alpina*, a small, spreading, prostrate shrub, is covered with a profusion of deep pink or cream-coloured, sweetly scented flowers. The little, 5–10 millimetre leaves are crowded together near the tips of the branchlets.

Yellow easterners

In the yellow rice-flower, *P. flava*, the arrangement and colour of its flowerheads make it one of the most attractive species native to South Australia, Victoria, New South Wales and Tasmania. It is an open wiry plant, flourishing in sandy heathland or damp forested areas, and reaching from 0.5–1.5 metres in height with very small, almost circular leaves set along the stems with geometrical precision. The tiny, bright yellow flowers, appearing in spring in small terminal clusters, are surrounded by four, large, yellow-green bracts, so that each flowerhead, only 10–15 millimetres across, looks exactly like a miniature Victorian posy. Male and female flowers are on different bushes, the female being rather less conspicuous.

The downy rice-flower, *P. octophylla*, widespread from South Australia through Victoria to New South Wales, also has yellow flowers but these are a much softer shade and are carried in large, nodding heads with eight short bracts. The small, grey-green leaves and the sweetly scented flowers are covered in fine hairs. Like the yellow rice-flower it is only a small shrub, less than 1 metre tall.

The largest flowerheads to be found among the *Pimelea* species are those of *P. spectabilis*. This is a small, upright shrub growing in the jarrah forests in the south-west of Western Australia and flowering in the spring. It has narrow, oblong leaves about 3 centimetres long and white to pink or cream flowers in clusters 5 centimetres across.

The pimelea daisy-bush is not a *Pimelea* but a bushy shrub about 1 metre tall with hairy, grey foliage similar to that of many rice-flowers. It is common in the drier regions, such as the mallee scrub, of most of the mainland States. In late winter and spring it is covered with white daisy-type flowers. Its botanical name is *Olearia pimeleoides*. ●

PALMS—ECONOMIC RESOURCE

Tree of life, says the Bible

Alexandra palm in flower.

ANT – R&D Keller

The Bible refers to the palm as the Tree of Life. Some 5500 years ago palm trees were grown for shade, beauty, food and oil. Of course, palms are much older than that — fossils estimated to be 120 million years old have been found, making them the oldest of all flowering plants.

Spectacular as they may be, palm trees also play a practical part in the economy of many countries: throughout Asia, Central America and parts of Africa, palm is a valuable raw material essential for economic survival.

Although usually associated with idyllic tropical settings, palms are found throughout Asia, Africa, North and South America, and the islands of the Pacific and Indian Oceans. Twenty-one genera are indigenous to Australia. Palms grow in rainforests, on tropical coasts, on riverbanks and in cultivated regions, or stand majestically in the parks and streets of tropical and subtropical cities.

Palms are members of the large family Palmae (or Aracaceae). There are about 140 genera, divided into eight tribes, and consisting of some 2000 known species; new types are still being discovered in the jungles of Central and South America. They are found mainly in tropical and subtropical regions with annual rainfalls of over 500 millimetres.

Palms vary in size from the tiny ground-living *Serenoas* of Florida to the giant wax palms of the Andes which reach 60 metres. Some, like the date palms, are tall and straight; some, like the coconut trees, are curved; some are low and shrubby; and others, like the Malayan rattans, are climbing vines.

Cabbage-tree palm

Much of northern Australia has the warm climatic conditions and heavy rainfall in which palms thrive. Australia boasts some 50 indigenous species, of which 40 are found north of the Tropic of Capricorn. There are no native palms in the south of Western Australia, in South Australia or Tasmania, and the most southerly species is the cabbage tree palm, *Livistona australis*.

The genus *Livistona* was named in honour of Baron Livingstone who established the botanical gardens near Edinburgh in Scotland in the 19th century. Cabbage tree palms were common in the temperate coastal rainforests that once grew in areas such as the Illawarra in New South Wales. Their tall slender trunks grow to 25 metres in height and are topped by a dense crown of shiny, fan-shaped leaves.

The leaves were used by early settlers to make baskets and broad-brimmed hats. The tender bud or 'cabbage' at the top of this and other palms was used for food by Aboriginals and by sailors, who were always short of fresh vegetables; it was eaten raw, boiled or baked in ashes.

Livistona mariae is a shorter, stouter palm which grows only at Palm Valley in the Finke River basin, southwest of Alice Springs in the Northern Territory.

Discovered and named by Ernest Giles in 1872, this valley in the MacDonell Ranges is now a flora and fauna reserve and a popular tourist attraction. The existence of these ancient palms in the arid heart of Australia indicates that the centre of the continent was once much more lush and well-watered than it is today. Their survival now depends upon the palms' capacity to soak up water from the sand of the Finke riverbed.

Kentias and rattons

Among the best-known palms in the Areceae tribe are the species of *Howea*, also known as Kentias, which are natives of Lord Howe Island At one time, the island's prosperity depended on collecting the seeds, which rarely set, for world markets.

Several rattans or climbing palms are native to Australia and belong to the large genus *Calamus* of the tribe *Calameae*. This is one of the largest genera with some 300 species, and its members occur throughout the world. The climbing palm is actually a scrambler which hoists itself up by hooks on its leaves which it attaches to other forest plants and trees. The long, thin, flexible stem can reach 30 metres, but much of it lies in coils on the ground.

The Australian rattans are called lawyer vines or lawyer canes. *C. muelleri* grows in the forests of northern New South Wales and southern Queensland. It uses the many sharp spikes on its leaf sheaths to pull itself up, often causing impassable thickets.

Several exotic palm species have been introduced into Australia and are now naturalised. The coconut probably arrived from New Guinea and was being used by Torres Strait Islanders

Fan palm, *Licuala muelleri*, has large circular leaves which look as though they have been trimmed with a pair of serrated-edge scissors. Found in Queensland, fan palms are regarded as Australia's best palm. Suitable for indoors.

Lawyer vine frond (also known as yellow thorny Mary and wait-a while), *Calamus moti*, is a climbing species found in tropical rainforests of northern Queensland. Named thorny Mary because of the sharp spines on the fronds and stem. Suitable for potting; stems grow to about one metre.

Fruit of the fishtail lawyer vine, *Calamus caryotoides*.

Possibly the most popular of all garden and indoor palms is the Alexandra, also known as feather and king palm, *Archontophoenix alexandrae*. This palm will grow to 13 metres and the underside of the leaves are silvery-grey, the flowers cream and the fruit red.

along the shores of northern Australia long before the coming of white settlers. The date palm, so useful in the Middle East, has also been introduced but more for decorative than commercial purposes. The water coconut, *Nipa fruticans*, is a strange palm which grows in river swamps and marshes from Sri Lanka to Malaysia, New Guinea and northern Queensland. It bears large seeds and hanging fruit up to 30 centimetres in diameter. The leaves are used to make mats, hats and for thatching native huts.

Closely related to grasses

Despite their variety, palms as a group have several distinguishing features. They are more closely related to grasses, bamboo, lilies, orchids, tulips and irises than to most trees.

Unlike most flowering trees, palm trunks do not have a layer of bark covering an inner layer of multiplying cells, nor do they add annual growth rings of wood and bark to the outside of their trunks. The tough, fibrous hide gives remarkable strength to the upright stem which, combined with its flexibility, enables the palm to withstand high winds and cyclones.

Palms have a unique root system — the primary root has no capacity to increase in diameter and has only a limited branching ability. The stem is surmounted by a crown of evergreen

Black palm, *Normanbya normanbyi*, is suitable for indoor and tub planting and in its natural habitat in Queensland will grow to 25 metres. The fruit of this palm is orange-red.

Two month old coconut seedling.

Cabbage tree palm, *Livistona australis* (left), is described as being 'a very stately palm' growing to 25 metres. The trunk is slender and its leaves are fan-like. Suitable for garden, indoor and tub planting.

An *Archontophoenix* palm.

Detail shot of the fan-like leaves of the cabbage tree palm (left).

leaves or fronds which vary tremendously in size. The blade or terminal portion of the leaf, which determines the leaf shape, is either fan-like (palmate) or feather-like (pinnate). Palmate leaves form a handsome fan shape with separate leaflets radiating from a central region like spread fingers. Pinnate leaves have a central rib with leaflets branching off on both sides like a feather. Spines or prickles are sometimes present on parts of the leaf stalk.

The fruits vary from small berries to the huge double coconut, some 122 centimetres in circumference, of the Seychelles palm, *Lodoicea maldavica*. They come in all colours and some like coconuts, are encased in a thick bark or fibre cover.

96

Bay Picture Library

Bay Picture Library

These palms in Palm Valley in Northern Territory are evidence that before the desert there was lush vegetation in this area. The palms, *Livistona mariae*, are now regarded as very rare (above).

Kentia or thatch palm of Lord Howe Island (left).

This palm, *Corypha elata*, is now very rare and is apparently now only found along a few rivers in tropical north Queensland (right).

ANT C&D Frith

AQUATIC PLANTS

Cool, floating blossoms fed by water

The origin of water plants for landscape design can be traced back 7000 years to China where water was considered an integral, aesthetic part of garden creation. In Australia there are many aquatic plants occurring naturally and many of these have been introduced to suburban gardens and rockeries.

Although the greater part of the Australian continent is arid, the coastal areas are rich in waterways, lagoons and billabongs together with man-made reservoirs, irrigation and drainage channels. These areas support a wealth of aquatic plants many of which are not confined to Australia but may be found in similar conditions throughout the world.

The pink waterlily or sacred lotus of India (*Nelumbo nucifera*) is at home in the quiet freshwater lagoons of tropical Australia but is also found from southern USSR eastwards through southern Asia into China, Japan and Papua New Guinea.

In cultivation it travels much further south and fine specimens may be seen in the Adelaide Botanic Gardens. The roots and thick underground stems are submerged in the muddy bottom but, unlike most other waterlilies, the large circular leaves are usually held above the surface of the water. They may be as much as 60 centimetres or more across and look rather like umbrellas, blown inside out.

The pink waterlily prefers deep water, the leaf stalks often reaching 1.5 metres in length, while the flower stalks are even longer, holding the big fragrant blooms clear of the foliage. The flowers are solitary, up to 25 centimetres in diameter, and the numerous pink petals surround a cluster of yellow stamens. Just occasionally, white flowered plants are produced.

The stems of both leaves and flowers are kept buoyant by elongated, air-filled canals within them. When the petals fall, the peanut-like fruits are left to ripen in a distinctive, inverted cone-shaped structure, each one held loosely in a depression on the flattened upper surface. This receptacle becomes hard and dry, eventually turning upside down to release the fruit which float away.

Native to the tropical north, the giant waterlily, *Nymphaea gigantea* makes a dramatic display in water gardens.

A substitute for coffee beans

The seeds, one to each fruit, remain viable for incredibly long periods, one is know to have ger-

The heron bristle rush, *Chorizandra cymbaria* occurs in all states except South Australia. It is hardy and suitable for moist areas around a pond.

ANT G. Cheers

The tall, spike rush, *Eleocharis sphacelata* grows wild in many open ponds, lakes and billabongs. It will also survive in wet soil.

ANT Keith Vagg

The lotus flower, *Nelumbo nucifera* produces exquisite flowers on the surface of the water. It is a vigorous plant and suitable only in frost-free locations.

Bay Picture Library

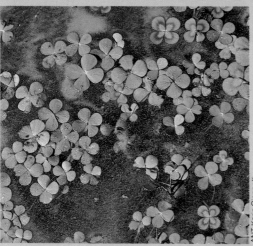

Reminiscent of four-leaf clover, the water fern, *Marsilea mutica* is a hardy plant, often used in cold water aquariums.

ANT Karin Ciannelli

minated after 237 years! Both fruits and creeping underground stems are edible, either raw or cooked. The explorer Leichhardt tried the former as a substitute for coffee beans and found them 'most excellent'.

Another splendid aquatic plant, the giant or native waterlily (*Nymphaea gigantea*) is native to the northern tropics of Australia and the eastern regions of Queensland and New South Wales as far south as the Clarence River. Unlike the lotus, outside Australia, it is found only in Papua New Guinea.

It flourishes in deep water, anchored to the thick, muddy bottom of sheltered pools and streams by fibrous roots and short upright tubers. The long, hollow leaf stalks, which were used by the aborigines as underwater breathing tubes, carry floating, dark green, rounded leaves as much as 75 centimetres across and with evenly spaced, sharply raised teeth on the margin.

In summer and autumn, the flowers are held high above the floating foliage. They are variable in size, sometimes even larger than those of the pink waterlily, with a central mass of yellow stamens and numerous lilac-blue petals, and occasionally white ones.

The flowers have no perfume. They open by day but close at night often trapping insects which help to pollinate them. As the flowers fade they are drawn below the water by spiral contractions of the stems. When ripe, the seeds are released from the soft, rounded fruit and float for several days before sinking.

The blue or Cape waterlily (*Nymphaea capensis*), a close relative of the giant waterlily, was introduced to Australia from Africa and is now often seen in southern Queensland and the north and central coastal regions of New South Wales. The leaves are smaller than those of its native cousin and without the sharp teeth while the normally smaller blue flowers are scented and have narrower, pointed petals. Rare white forms are sometimes seen.

Celery-like and totally edible

Almost every part of these two plants is said to be edible, the fruits being roasted before the seeds are eaten while the stalks, with the outer skin removed, are chewed like celery. Pink, red and white flowered hybrids and cultivars of other *Nymphaea* species are often grown.

Another group of Australian aquatic plants extends much further south, from the tropics into New South Wales and Victoria. These belong to the genus *Nymphoides* and include the marshworts and fringed waterlilies whose short-lived, white or yellow, fringed flowers and floating leaves, carpet still lagoons or dawdling waterways and channels where water may be up to 1.5 metres deep.

One of the best known, the wavy marshwort (*N. crenata*), buries its roots in the muddy bottom sending out long-stalked, waxy, round to heart-shaped glossy leaves to float on the surface and elongated, branching stems, one metre or more in length, to hang just below it.

At intervals along the stems, clusters of floating roots and three or four short-stalked, floating leaves are produced. From spring to autumn, clusters of long-stemmed, solitary yellow flowers with four or five, winged, fringed lobes appear.

After pollination, the flower stems curl down to allow the pale, shining seeds to ripen under water. This characteristic distinguishes this genus from *Villarsia* with which they are often confused.

Popular in garden pools

Other species of *Nymphoides* such as the entire marshwort or fringed waterlily (*N. geminata*), which is found in the swamps and fast moving streams of high altitudes, carry their short-stalked, yellow flowers in pairs along a small side branch. The water snowflake, (*N. indica*) whose range extends into tropical regions across the Old World, bears heavily fringed, pure white or white and yellow blooms. The marshworts are sometimes seen in garden pools.

Widespread in all the mainland states except for the northern parts of Western Australia, the swamp lily (*Ottelia ovalifolia*), is found not only in calm backwaters and slow-moving streams, but also in rice crops and stock tanks where its floating foliage may cover the entire surface, detering the stock from drinking.

When young, the swamp lily with its roots fixed in the bottom, produces a tuft of fine-textured, ribbon-like leaves but as the plant matures these are replaced by fleshy, long-stalked floating leaves. The flowers are of two kinds but both are bi-sexual. In summer, open cup-shaped blooms appear, held above the dark, shining foliage. Enclosed at first in fleshy, dark green, ridged bracts they open to expose three creamy white petals conspicuously creased longitudinally and splashed with maroon at the base. A cluster of showy yellow stamens fills the centre.

Once these blooms are cross-pollinated from other flowers, the stems curve down to allow the seed to ripen under-water. Other smaller flowers remain below the water, enclosed in a bract which does not open. They are self-pollinating. The seeds of both types of flowers are fertile.

An introduced pest from Brazil

One of the most beautiful but destructive water plants, the water hyacinth, (*Eichhornia crassipes*), is not an Australian native but was introduced from Brazil in 1895. The one metre tall, free-

The attractive frog mouth, *Philydrum lanuginosum* is often sited at a pool's edge. It will grow in damp soil in full sun or part shade.

The nardoo, *Marsilea drummondii* often grows as a terrestial on the edge of inland lakes. It was once gathered by Aborigines and ground into flour.

The majestic white waterlily, *sp. Nymphoides* produces its flowers in clusters from a node just under the leaf. It is often used in aquariums.

The yellow marshwort, *Nymphoides hydrocharloides* inhabits ponds, lagoons and other watercourses of northern Australia.

ANT D.A. Henley

ANT G.B. Baker

Although decorative, the water hyacinth, *Eichhornia crassipes* can often run wild, blocking drains and clogging irrigation channels.

These paperbark trees, *Melaleuca leucadendron* (left) inhabit swamp areas of northern Australia. Their attractive cream flowers have a delightful perfume.

floating clumps of rounded, waxy leaves on swollen stems and crowded spikes of gorgeous, lavender-blue flowers soon escaped from garden pools to natural and manmade waterways.

The rapidity with which these plants increase to become impenetrable mats causes tremendous problems; a single plant can cover 600 square metres in one season. They slow or stop water traffic, block drainage and irrigation channels, ruin fishing grounds and even cause bridges to collapse with the result that they have been declared noxious weeds in southern states.

Efforts to find some economic use for the water hyacinth have been unsuccessful although cattle and pigs will eat the leaves. Chemical control can be negated by reinfestation from long lived seeds and at present hopes of controlling the water hyacinth are pinned to biological control using a weevil and a moth from South America.

TEA-TREES

Tough but pretty

Denise Greig

With their aromatic foliage, small leaves and hard, woody seed capsules, the tea-trees, *Leptospermum*, are typical plants of the Australian bushland community. Like the gum trees they are part of the myrtle family, *Myrtaceae*, which means they are also related to the bottlebrushes, *Callistemon*, fringe myrtles, *Calytrix*, wax flowers, *Chamelaucium*, and paperbarks, *Melaleuca*.

It was from the *Leptospermum* trees that leaves were taken to be used as a substitute for tea by Captain Cook and his crew when they were camped at Dusky Bay, New Zealand, during his first voyage. The incident is referred to in his account of his second voyage, *A Voyage towards the South Pole*, published in 1777. An accompanying illustration of the plant from which the leaves were picked shows it to have been *L. scoparium*. This species is common to both Australia and New Zealand and is the parent of many of the lovely garden cultivars.

The common name of tea-tree is sometimes spelt 'ti' but this is the Maori name for the New Zealand cabbage-tree, *Cordyline australis*, so it should not be used for *Leptospermum* species. The 40 or so species of *Leptospermum*,

Leptospermum scoparium var. *rotundifolium* grows up to two metres and spreads three metres across. It has shiny leaves and white to deep pink flowers. It is particularly suited to hybridization.

are evergreen trees and shrubs with extensive and varied habitats. Different species are suited to harsh coastal conditions, mountainous terrain, poor rocky soils, sandy heaths or high rainfall.

The trees are very attractive to bees as the blooms are filled with pollen or nectar. The honey produced from them has a distinctive but not very pleasing flavour. It is thick and jelly-like, making it difficult to extract from the combs.

Their structure

Their leaves are simple and arranged alternately along the branches, a fact which helps distinguish them from the *Baeckeas*, whose flowers are similar but whose leaves are opposite. In many species the oil glands are clearly visible.

The flowers of most species range in colour from white to pink or red. They have five sepals fused into a five-lobed cup, the calyx, and five spreading petals, circular or sometimes wedge-shaped, arranged evenly around the rim. There is a single ring of 20 to 30 short stamens. In some species the flowers are solitary, in others, clustered on short spurs that rise from the leaf axils near the tips of the branches. The five-celled seed cases are hard, woody capsules which, like those of many other Australian plants, remain on the shrub indefinitely, opening to release their seeds only when split by the heat of bush fires. The seeds are numerous, light brown, fine and elongated, giving rise to the generic, botanical name *Leptospermum*, from the Greek: 'leptos' meaning slender and 'sperma' meaning seed.

The coastal tea-tree

One of the largest and most widespread of the tea-trees, the coastal tea-tree, *L. laevigatum*, grows as a dense bush on the sandhills and sandy heaths of the eastern and southern coasts of the continent. Its roots act as valuable sand binders and its branches and foliage withstand the salt-laden storms, protecting the more tender plants further inland. In such exposed positions it may be a small twisted tree or a misshapen, multi-stemmed shrub up to six metres tall but in sheltered gullies it has been known to reach 12 metres.

The grey-green, oval to oblong leaves are one to two centimetres long and the solitary, white flowers, about two centimetres across, have widely-spaced petals which appear from early spring to summer. The bark is deeply furrowed and the timber, which is tough and long-lasting, at one time provided the wood for fashionable, rustic garden seats. Today it is used for brush fences. Trees of this and other species make tall straight saplings if grown in

Denise Greig

Leptospermum scoparium 'Lambethii' is a popular cultivar but it is prone to both scale insects and disfiguring black smut, both of which can be treated.

Aust. Transparency Lib.

The coastal tea-tree, *Leptospermum laevigatum*, is remarkably hardy. Resistant to salt spray and accustomed to sandy soil, it provides good screening and is frequently used for windbreaks.

protected sites and under these cultivated conditions Aboriginals used them for spears.

Manuka tea-tree

Another widespread species is the variable *L. scoparium*, known in New Zealand as manuka. Often it is a spreading three-metre shrub with narrow, stiff, pointed leaves about one centimetre long, which can be seen on heathlands of the eastern mainland states as well as South Australia, Tasmania and New Zealand. In high rainfall forests, where it sometimes grows, it becomes more tree-like, reaching twice that height. The solitary flowers are small, only one centimetre across, white, occasionally tinged with pink. They appear in spring and summer.

A variety of this tea-tree, *L. s. var. rotundifolium* (syn. *L. rotundifolium*), with much larger flowers, two and a half centimetres across, and glossy, rounded leaves six millimetres in diameter, is found in New South Wales. The flowers may be white through to deep mauve or rosy pink. Garden cultivars of *L. scoparium* include 'Red Damask', 'Sunraysia', the various forms of 'Nicholii' and the multicoloured, winter-flowering 'Lambethii'.

Cultivated tea-trees

The peach-blossom tea-tree, *L. squarrosum*, is another species that is often cultivated. Its natural habitat is along the streams of the central coast of New South Wales, spreading into the south coast, the edge of the tablelands and northwards as far as Queensland. The pale to

In autumn and winter the peach blossom tea-tree, *Leptospermum squarrosum*, produces clusters of flowers all along the old wood while leaves grow from the new.

This cultivar, *Leptospermum lanigerum* var. *macrocarpum*, is a small scrambling tea-tree well suited to rockeries. It has large attractive pink or white flowers and dark green oblong leaves.

Leptospermum sericeum is a Western Australian species of tea-tree, requiring good drainage and full sun to produce its usual profusion of pink flowers.

deep pink flowers, one and a half centimetres wide, are carried in abundance along the slightly pendulous branches from late spring to summer. The foliage is variable in shape but it is always small, stiff and prickly.

Unusual tea-trees

Not all tea-trees make large shrubs or small trees. The mountains of Tasmania are home to the creeping tea-tree, *L. rupestre*, which, finding shelter among the rocks, is generally prostrate but occasionally grows into a more upright plant. The thick, shining leaves, each with a fringe of white hairs, are crowded together and the solitary white flowers are produced abundantly in mid-summer.

Once classified as a *Kunzea*, *L. phylicoides* bears its atypical flowers in summer. The bush is tall, up to five metres, with narrow, two-and-a-half-centimetre leaves. The numerous,

white flowers are small, about one centimetre in diameter but the prominent anthers give them a fringed appearance quite different from the normal tea-tree blooms. The plant is common in the New South Wales tablelands, the Australian Capital Territory and Victoria and is occasionally seen in South Australia and Queensland.

Tea-trees whose leaves or buds are covered with silky or woolly hairs include *L. brevipes*, the woolly tea-tree, *L. lanigerum*, and the silky tea-tree, *L. myrsinoides*. *L. brevipes* is a large, rather weeping shrub up to four metres in height, found in the heathland and lightly-timbered areas of southeast Queensland and the eastern half of New South Wales and Victoria. The white flowers, with their well-spaced rounded petals, appear in spring or early summer and the two-centimetre, oblong leaves are covered with short, silky hairs.

The woolly tea-tree, often found in damp or swampy regions of Tasmania as well as the eastern states and South Australia, is a shrub with many forms. The shape may change from a spreading three-metre shrub in open country to that of an upright 18-metres tree in wet forests. The leaves are variable in form but the foliage and young shoots are covered with silky hairs as are the flower buds and young seed capsules.

The silky tea-tree is an erect shrub growing up to two metres tall. Its numerous spring flowers are white or pink and the calyces are covered with fine hairs. Like so many of the tea-trees it flourishes in sandy heathland in South Australia, Victoria and New South Wales.

A most unusual tea-tree, rarely seen until its recent introduction as an ornamental garden plant, is *L. fabricia* from the Iron Ranges of Northern Queensland. It is a large upright shrub, which often reaches to four metres. It has oblong, three-centimetre long leaves and, unlike its southern counterparts, its abundance of flowers are bright yellow. The bark contains a resin which was used by Aboriginals of the area in their bark paintings. It was released by heating and rubbed into the surface before decoration was applied.

Endemic species

As with so many native plants Western Australia has its own examples of tea trees. The largest-flowered of the ten endemic species is the silver tea tree, *L. sericeum*, which is confined to a small area around Esperance and the islands off the coast. Like those species mentioned above the foliage of this one to two metre shrub is silky haired. The very large flowers, up to five centimetres across, are shaded from pale to deep pink, opening in spring.

WATTLES

The largest family of native flora in Australia — one species features on our national coat of arms.

Queensland silver wattle, *Acacia podalyriifolia*, has distinctive silvery-grey foliage as well as the familiar "fluffy-ball" yellow flowers.

ANT R & D Keller

The wattles, *Acacia* spp., form the largest family of native flora in Australia and include well over 600 known species — more than half the entire world-wide family which spreads through many warm climate countries.

Wattles grow naturally in almost all parts of Australia from the arid inland to the rainforests of Tasmania and the alpine stretches of the Snowy Mountains. Some are drought resistant enduring the harsh conditions of the deserts while others flourish along riverbanks and watercourses.

In size they range from the tall blackwoods, *A. melanoxylon*, reaching 30 metres or more in moist and sheltered gullies of eastern and southern Australia, to the Western Australian *A. pilosa* which is rarely more than 20 centimetres in height.

Origin of name

The botanical name *Acacia* comes from the Greek word for 'thorny' which it justly deserves: the first named species, the North African gum arabic tree, *Acacia arabica*, has fearsome 5–7 centimetre long spines. The common name 'wattle' may come from 'wattah', the Aboriginal word for some of the trees or, even more likely, from the use made of the pliable branches by the early settlers to build their wattle-and-daub huts.

No matter how the genus derived its common name, many of the Aboriginal names for individual species such as gidgee, *A. cambagei*, wirilda, *A. retinodes*, eumong, *A. stenophylla*, and yarran, *A. homalophylla*, have passed into current use while others like myall, *A. pendula*, mulga, *A. aneura*, and brigalow, *A. harpophylla* are now used to describe whole areas where these trees abound.

Varying leaf stalks

While all wattle seedlings have divided, fern-like or feathery leaves (technically known as pinnate), as they mature more than half of the species replace these with modified leaf-stalks (phyllodes) which carry out the functions of true foliage. These phyllodes vary in size and shape and may be needle-like, long and narrow, straight or sickle-shaped, oval, triangular or wedge-shaped.

Yellow globular-headed flowers of the blackwood, *A. melanoxylon*, the largest of the wattles.

ANT G. Cheers

Wirilda, *A. retinodes*, is unusual for a wattle as it can produce flowers at any time of the year and is not restricted to a particular season.

Ivy Hansen

A woodland of mulga, *A. aneura*, in central Australia — there are few ecosystems that are not populated with wattles.

R. Jenkins

A closer view of the bright yellow ball-shaped flowers of the Queensland silver wattle, *A. podalyriifolia*.

Bay Picture Library

Commonly called prickly moses, the wattle *A. verticillata*, has sharply-pointed fern-like leaves.

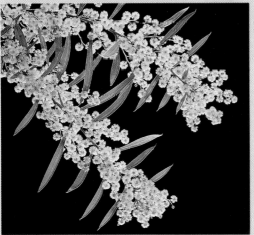

Golden wattle, *A. pycnantha*, displays an abundance of fluffy-ball shaped golden flowers. It is the floral emblem of the Australian Commonwealth.

A shrub often seen on coastal heaths, the sweet scented wattle, *A. suaveolens*, has pale creamy blooms.

Sydney golden wattle, *A. longifolia*, has flowers growing along spikes.

The largest phyllodes, often 30 centimetres long, are found on the eumong or river-cooba and on *A. dunnii*, a slender tree growing along the Victoria River in northern Australia. In many species, like the well-known Queensland silver wattle, *A. podalyriifolia*, the foliage is silvery-grey but in others such as the pale flowered, feather-leaved cedar wattles, *A. elata*, it is dark green.

Prickles, thorns or sharply pointed phyllodes are found in some wattles. The kangaroo thorn, *A. paradoxa*, (syn. *A. armata*), is sometimes used for barrier hedges because of the pairs of sharp spikes growing at the base of the phyllodes while both *A. ulicifolia* (syn. *A. juniperina*) and *A. verticillata* have such sharply pointed phyllodes that they go by the common name of prickly moses.

Gold yellow and orange flowers

Wattle flowers are very small with five tiny petals and numerous conspicuous stamens. They are arranged in either globular heads like the familiar fluffy balls seen on the golden wattle, *A. pycnantha*, which forms part of the national coat of arms, or along spikes as in the Sydney golden wattle, *A. longifolia*, a bushy shrub or small tree common in eastern states.

Their colour ranges from the pale creamy blooms of the sweet-scented wattle, *A. suaveolens*, which bears its fragrant blossom in the cold weather, through all shades of yellow to the bright golden balls of the popular Cootamundra wattle, *A. baileyana*, and the deep, almost orange flowers of the Western Australian golden wattle or orange wattle *A. saligna*, (syn. *A. cyanophylla*).

In the latter species, the flowers are borne in such profusion in late spring that they weigh down the branchlets. The flowers are distinctly perfumed but may cause hay fever among those allergic to the large quantities of pollen they contain.

Many species flower in spring but others bloom in summer, autumn or winter while a few like wirilda, *A. retinodes*, may produce flowers at any time of the year and are cultivated for this very reason.

Seeds in pods

Wattles' seeds are carried in legumes, or pods, which dry out and split along both sides to release their seeds. The size, shape and texture of the pods are as variable as the shape of the leaves:

The cootamundra wattle, *A. baileyana*, has many gold to yellow ball-shaped flowers. More common in the south.

A detail of acacia seeds in their pod. Wattles are so versatile they can grow equally well alongside rainforests, in sand along beaches, and in dusty, arid soil.

Proof of the wattle's range of habitats: here on a coastal dune in Gippsland, Victoria. This coast species, *A. sophorae*, occurs in such habitats in Tasmania and eastern Borders.

The blackwood, *A. melanoxylon*, is a good timber tree from Queensland south to Tasmania — normally where rainfall exceeds 600 mm. It grows to a height of 30 metres.

they may be straight or coiled, flat or cylindrical, smooth, polished or hairy.

The seeds have tough coats and retain their viability for many years, some have even been known to germinate when almost 100 years old.

In natural conditions the seeds are often released from their dormancy by bushfires; cut when cultivated they need some form of treatment, such as soaking in hot water, nicking or abrading to quicken their germination.

Food value

While it is known that the Aboriginals ate the roasted seeds of some wattles, including those of eumong and coast myall, *A. longifolia* var. *sophorae*, and that sheep browse on both pods and seeds of prickly moses, *A. farnesiana*, and gidgee, *A. cambagei*, without ill effect, many of the pods and/or seeds are poisonous and should not be eaten experimentally.

Research into the food value of these seeds is being carried out and some have been found to be rich in protein but many species have not yet been tested.

The gum, however, which oozes from the trees in translucent amber or reddish-brown masses is edible and can be sucked or soaked in water to turn it into a jelly-like mass. The taste is slight except in the darker coloured ones which being high in tannin tend to be astringent. In non-Australian species this gum is used in making adhesives but that of Australian species is not suitable for this purpose.

Commercial properties

Some wattle timber is used commercially. Blackwood, *A. melanoxylon*, is milled for top quality furniture and veneers where its beautifully patterned grain can be displayed. The strongly marked mulga and gidgee are turned and polished for tourist souvenirs as well as being used, together with ironwood, *A. excelsa* and brigalow, *A. harpophylla*, for more utilitarian purposes such as fences, stockyards and mining timbers where strength is needed.

Wattle bark of some species is high in tannin and considered among the best in the world for tanning leather. Almost all wattle makes good firewood.

Wattle trees are also popular as ornamental plants because of their fast growth and spectacular floral display. Unfortunately they are relatively short-lived and prone to attack by pests and diseases such as borers and gall fungus. ●

Douglas Baglin

Killers and Curatives

Plants are not always what they seem. Masters of disguise to the uninitiated, they can trap, strangle, lure, poison and purify. Some possess chemical properties which are deadly while others have legendary healing qualities. Many of them are commonly used in the manufacture of pharmaceuticals, pesticides and cosmetics. It is not always easy to identify these plants, so if you are thinking of dabbling in a little herbalism proceed with caution.

109

PLANTS WITH HEALING POWERS: BUSH MEDICINE

Australia has some 500 plant species, all growing wild, which are now used for medicinal purposes either here or overseas.

ANT I.R. McCann

The leaves of the native paperbark trees were often chewed for their aromatic qualities in treating head colds.

The bark of the wattle, due to its tannin content, was brewed by white settlers and used mainly for gastric and intestinal disorders.

The bark of the black wattle was once exported to Britain and listed as a medicinal in the *British Pharmacopoeia*.

The bark of the sassafras, found in rainforests was used to make a tonic drink which was exported and marketed in Britain.

The kangaroo apple (far left) is an important source of the steroid solasodine which is used in oral contraceptives.

Driven by instinct, even the earliest man often found a cure in some natural plants and herbs for his ailments. It is hardly surprising, really, that from this hesitant search a vast pharmaceutical industry has developed.

Aboriginals have used many different types of plants to cure their ills for thousands of years. Early European settlers soon learnt, through necessity, about the healing properties of native plants, and many of their remedies have remained in use.

More recently, scientific investigation has led to important new discoveries of therapeutic Australian plants. The majority of native plants with known or potential medical use grow in Queensland, particularly in the tropical rainforests.

Modern research has proved that many Australian plants used for remedies in the past do, in fact, have therapeutic value. It appears that the usefulness of some plants, however, may have been largely psychological; in the case of Aboriginal therapies, the accompanying use of magic was often a powerful factor.

Tannin, latex useful

There are certain major types of medicinal substances to be found in plants. Australian flora has an abundance of plants with oil glands, such as eucalypts and tea-trees, which are described as aromatic.

When the leaves are crushed the oil evaporates and may be breathed in; this has been found particularly useful in respiratory ailments. (A number of oils have been proved to have antimicrobial action.)

Tannins, usually occurring in bark, are found in many plants; acting as an astringent, they draw tissues together and are useful in treating the inflamed mucous membranes characteristic of colds and intestinal infections.

Latex, the pale fluid which exudes if a stem or leaf of certain plants is broken, often contains enzymes which digest protein and are used in the removal of skin eruptions such as corns and warts.

Then there are the alkaloids, which generally have a bitter taste and include such valuable drugs as quinine and codeine.

Aboriginal medicine

The Aboriginals, with their deep and intricate understanding of their natural environment, discovered and used many plants with therapeutic qualities.

A survey in the late 1960s found that at least 124 species of native plants were considered by Aboriginals to have medicinal value. As Australia is such a huge continent, with varying climate, topography, soil and other factors creating different botanical regions, particular ailments were treated with different plants in different regions.

Many aromatic plants were used as palliatives for colds, coughs and chest complaints; these included several eucalyptus species, the young leaves of which were generally rubbed, squeezed and soaked in water until they produced a green liquid.

The new leaves of certain melaleuca (paperbark) trees were often simply chewed for their aromatic qualities in treating head colds.

Coughs and colds were also treated by several species of acacia (wattle), the bark and roots — containing tannin — being made into an infusion or soaked to make a syrup or liquid. Headaches were generally treated by sniffing the crushed leaves of certain aromatic plants.

Fruit leaves useful

Native figs of the genus *Ficus* were used for the latex, generally milky in appearance, which exudes from their broken leaves or stems; this was applied to small wounds and infections such as ringworm.

Among other plants used medicinally by the Aboriginals is a species of pittosporum known as meemeei (*Pittosporum phylliraeoides*) which is a small tree with willow-like foliage found in dry regions.

Brews of the leaves or fruit were taken internally or applied externally for a variety of ills including internal pains, sprained limbs and skin irritations such as eczema.

In certain parts of New South Wales, the warmed leaves of the tree were held against a mother's breast to induce the first flow of milk following childbirth.

European experience

Early European settlers in bush areas, often out of reach of professional medical help, also developed a considerable knowledge of plant remedies to assist them in times of sickness or injury.

In some cases plants brought from their northern homelands were cultivated for this purpose. Many also learnt about the medicinal qualities of Australian native plants: either through communication with Aboriginals or through experimentation with plants resembling herbs of the northern hemisphere.

Many of the remedies developed by the early settlers are still used today, particularly by bush dwellers or those who follow alternative lifestyles. These include treatments for complaints such as colds, coughs, skin infections and diarrhoea.

Broken leaves or stems of native fig trees exude a milky latex which was often applied to small wounds and infections such as ringworm.

The leaves of the red stringybark contain the pigment rutin which is used to treat capillary fragility and as a preservative for other medicinals.

A gum taken from the bark of eucalypts contains tannin which is used as an astringent in the treatment of throat infections.

The kino or gum of the giant river red gum trees was used in the preparation of cough lozenges.

The geebung, a coastal heathland shrub has been found to be active against salmonella typhi, the bacteria which causes typhoid fever.

The common sneezeweed was used by Aboriginals for heavy colds while bush settlers made an infusion with the plant to relieve eye inflammations.

Prickly geebung is another variety of *Persoonia* which has recently been the subject of tests carried out by scientists.

A close-up of the bunches of fruit produced by *Persoonia pinifolia*, a hardy coastal shrub with medicinal properties.

The bark of the wattle (*Acacia*) was used by white settlers mainly for gastric and intestinal disorders, rather than for colds and coughs as did the Aboriginals. An astringent due to its tannin content, wattle bark was generally brewed with boiling water as a remedy for dysentery or diarrhoea.

The bark of the species known as black wattle, *Acacia decurrens*, was at one time exported to Britain and was included in the *British Pharmacopoeia*. The kino or 'gum' of wattle trees was dissolved in water to make a soothing syrup for inflamed mucous membranes.

Bark juice exported

The southern sassafras (*Atherosperma moschatum*), found in southern rainforests, was the first Australian species from which an alkaloid, atherospermine, was isolated. The bark of this tree was used to make a tonic drink or aperient and was exported to Britain where it was marketed as Victorian sassafras.

Several species of sneezeweed — which do actually make people sneeze! — were part of colonial medicine. These aromatic plants are members of the daisy family and are usually creeping in habit.

While the Aboriginals used the common sneezeweed, *Centipeda cunninghamii*, for heavy colds, white bush settlers used an infusion of the plant to relieve eye inflammation.

Another species known as the spreading sneezeweed, *Centipeda minima*, has a similar use. Following a Dr. Jockel's discovery of the effectiveness of sneezeweed in treating sandy blight, it was sold in tins as 'Magic Ophthalmia Cure'.

The colonial botanist, Ferdinand von Mueller, exhibited a snuff made from the seeds and leaves of the sneezeweed at the Intercolonial Exhibition in Melbourne in 1866.

Eucalyptus: a cure-all

A tea prepared from the asthma plant, *Euphorbia pilulifera*, was widely used in Queensland in the 1880s to relieve the symptoms of bronchitis and asthma. Recent research has shown that the tea relaxes the bronchioles and depresses respiration.

Eucalyptus oil was found in almost every medicine cupboard in colonial times, as well as being widely used overseas. Popular as a remedy for colds, the oil is often mixed with boiling water and used as an inhalant, or through a few drops on a handkerchief placed close to the nose for a similar purpose.

However, the oil is poisonous and people have died after drinking only a tablespoonful. Eucalypt leaves were often bruised in a billy of hot water to apply as a lotion for muscular aches; this remedy is still used by some people.

Kino or 'gum' from the bark of eucalypts contains tannin and is used as an astringent in the treatment of throat infections, diarrhoea and bleeding injuries.

The kino of eucalypts, particularly grey ironbarks, was for some years exported as "Botany Bay Kino". That of the river red gum, *Eucalyptus camaldulensis*, was used in cough lozenges.

Pioneer father and son

Systematic research into medicinal plants in Australia began in the second half of the nineteenth century. This was pioneered by Dr. Joseph Bancroft and his son, Dr. Thomas Bancroft, of Brisbane. By 1889 J. H. Maiden, the government botanist, was able to list 123 species with proven or potential medicinal use.

Although an emphasis on chemical synthesis developed in the early decades of the twentieth century, there was soon a return to natural drugs with the discovery of penicillin and other antibiotics produced by fungi, bacteria and other micro-organisms.

Since World War II there has been a great increase in the amount of research into medicinal plants in Australia. This is largely the result of a systematic survey of Australian plants conducted since 1944 by the Commonwealth Scientific and Industrial Research Organisation (CSIRO) in co-operation with Australian universities. Since 1960, more than 180 000 plants have been screened.

Cancer drug sought

Numerous Australian plants have been discovered to yield, or be capable of yielding, drugs valuable for their medicinal use.

The search for anti-cancer drugs, active in many countries at present, has had some particularly encouraging results in Australia. The bark of a medium-sized native tree known as the scrub yellowwood, *Bauerella simplicifolia*, has been found to contain a number of alkaloids, one of which — acronycine — has displayed antitumour activity over the widest range of cancers for any natural product tested.

A large fungus known as the giant puffball, *Calvatia gigantea*, contains an anti-cancer principle called calvacin which is currently under research.

Corkwood leaves now drugs

One of Australia's most important native medicinal plants is the duboisia or corkwood. The leaves of two species, *Duboisia myoporoides* and *D. leichhardtii*, are valuable sources of the alkaloid drugs, scopolamine (also known as hyoscine) and hyoscyamine.

Both drugs are used in ophthalmology to dilate the pupils of the eye and as sedatives. Duboisia trees were used during World War II, the drug scopolamine being of great value in preventing seasickness, during invasions by sea, and

The leaves of the wild tobacco plant, often called pituri, were chewed by Aboriginals to give a feeling of euphoria.

ANT I.R. McCann

The spreading sneezeweed in colonial times was effective in treating sandy blight and was sold in tins as 'Magic Ophthalmia Cure'.

ANT I.R. McCann

The puffball which is a large fungus, contains an anti-cancer substance called calvacin which is currently under research.

Denise Greig

in treating shell-shock. This led to the processing of *Duboisia* in Australia.

The pigment rutin is obtained from the leaves of two eucalypt species, *Eucalyptus macrorrhyncha* (red stringybark) and *E. youmanii* (Youman's stringybark). Rutin is used to treat capillary fragility and as a preservative for other medicinal preparations.

Three species of *Persoonia*, coastal heathland shrubs commonly known as geebung, have recently been shown to be active against salmonella typhi, the bacteria causing typhoid fever. Among other recent discoveries, it has been found that two species known as kangaroo apple, *Solanum aviculare* and *S. laciniatum*, are important sources of the steroid solasodine which is used in oral contraceptives.

BEWARE: POISONOUS PLANTS

A cautionary field guide to native and imported toxic seeds, fruits and leaves

Long before the first European arrivals, aboriginals were happily chewing fruits, seeds, roots, leaves and shoots either raw or cooked. But some had to be treated first, often by washing and cooking, to prevent any ill effects from the poisons they contained. They would also take advantage of these natural poisons to stun or kill fish, animals and even enemies. When the white settlers arrived they had no knowledge of local plants nor that some were poisonous and needed to be neutralised. They learnt by trial . . . and error.

The zamia palm of the cycad family, common in north Queensland's rainforests, has extremely toxic seeds which, if eaten, can damage the central nervous system.

ANT E.A. Pratt

The native burrawang palm, common along the New South Wales coast, has brilliant vermilion seeds which are extremely toxic.

While most wildlife thrives on natural vegetation, sheep and cattle that eat certain plants can die or be disabled depending on the condition of the animals and the stage of growth of the plants. Instances of poisoning are often most severe during flowering and seeding periods.

The poisonous elements most commonly found in native plants include alkaloids, cyanogenetic glycoside and saponins but still very little is known or documented about this aspect of many of our native flora. Enough information however is available about the seeds and ferns mentioned here to know that they should not be eaten in their raw state either by livestock or even humans, as the results could be unpleasant if not perhaps fatal.

Toxic cycads

One group of native plants, the cycads, are primitive, seed-bearing plants whose fossil record goes back 150 million years. A number of species have large, extremely toxic seeds unless the poison is neutralised by some method.

In most cases the poison causes gastrointestinal and liver injury, sometimes fatal, or it may damage the central nervous system resulting in 'zamia staggers' although this is more common if the foliage is eaten.

The *Cycas*, *Lepidozamia* and *Macrozamia* cycads are palm-like plants with single, thick trunks terminating in a crown of spreading fronds. Male cones contain pollen and are comparatively small but the female cones of the last two types, look like large pineapples and are made up of a number of egg-like seeds arranged around a central core.

The cones of the zamia, *Macrozamia moorei*, may be 80 centimetres long and weigh 15 kilogrammes, while those of the burrawang, *M. communis*, common in coastal New South Wales, are smaller, up to 45 centimetres long. The seeds of both species are brilliant vermillion.

The seeds of the *Cycas* are not arranged in this fashion but attached to pendulous stalk-like leaves springing from the top of the trunk.

Another cycad, *Bowenia*, has branching, underground stems; only the leaves, like overgrown maidenhair fronds, and the cones appear above the ground. The female cones are much smaller, only 10–15 centimetres long and the seeds are pale grey.

Explorers experiment

These seeds were probably the first Australian foods eaten by white men. In 1698 the Dutch explorer, Willem de Vlamingh — the first white man to see black swans and to name the Swan River accordingly — landed in Western Australia and sampled seeds of one of the cycads, *Macrozamia*, as did Captain Cook a hundred years later when he conducted experiments with

ANT Garry Werren

ANT Keith Williams

The scarlet seeds of the gidee-gidee or crab's eye contains an irritant and highly poisonous toxalbumin.

Stock losses are often attributed to the poisonous yellow rice flower which grows in all states including Tasmania.

Common bracken, one of the most widespread ferns of the Pteridium family can cause various forms of poisoning in livestock especially horses and pigs.

Common in eastern Australia, the mulga or rock fern has been known to cause stock deaths when eaten in large quantities.

The female cones of the zamia palm look like pineapples (left) and are made up of egg-like poisonous seeds arranged around a central core.

seeds from a plant later identified as *Cycas media*. The results were violently emetic and cathartic, indeed two of the pigs, which had eaten large quantities of the seeds, died.

Gidee-gidee giddyness

The gidee-gidee, *Abrus precatorius*, also called crab's eye, precatory bean, rosary pea and jequirity bean, is a scrambling perennial vine of the tropical north where it is found growing in sandy soil, often close by the beach. It has bright green, fern-like foliage and tight clusters of pink, pea-shaped flowers, occasionally white or purple. The five-centimetre long pods contain several rounded seeds about 6mm across with hard, glossy coats, black at the base, scarlet above.

The brilliant scarlet seeds of the gidee-gidee, widely used for necklaces by the Australian aborigines and the Pacific islanders, are especially attractive to children.

The seeds contain abrin, an irritant toxalbumin, which is extremely poisonous when taken intravenously or subcutaneously causing diarrhoea, repeated vomiting, weak, fast pulse, trembling hands and nausea. Although less toxic when taken orally, one seed chewed and swallowed has been known to cause death. However if the seed coat is unbroken the seed may pass harmlessly through the digestive system.

Tummy upset trees

The seeds of the candle-nut tree, *Aleurites moluccana*, are not nearly so poisonous although the tree belongs to the family *Euphorbiaceae* which contains many other plants renowned for their corrosive sap. The candle-nut tree grows in many Pacific islands and in southern Asia as well as in Australia. It can reach 18 metres in height with a spreading head, long-stalked, mostly lobed leaves covered with star-shaped hairs which give the tree a powdered look.

The loose clusters of small white flowers are followed by fleshy fruits up to 6 centimetres across containing hard stones rather like walnuts. These are rich in oil and, threaded on strips of palm leaf, are burnt as torches by Pacific islanders. The kernels, particularly if not ripe, can cause gastric upsets but are sometimes eaten without any ill effects. They do not appear to be as poisonous as the seeds of the tung-oil tree, *Aleurites fordii*, a native of China sometimes found in Australia.

Some wattles harmful

Although the seeds of many wattles are valuable as food some, such as those of the Georgina gidgee or gidyea, *Acacia georginae*, are harmful. This small, straggly tree, often multi-trunked, with narrow grey-green phyllodes (leaves) is found growing in north-west Queensland around the Georgina River and in nearby Northern Territory.

The ball-shaped yellow flowers are followed by flattened pods, 5–10 centimetres long and 2 centimetres wide, curled almost into a circle. The shape of the pods, and the flattened glossy brown seeds they contain, distinguish this wattle from the non-harmful gidgee, *Acacia cambagei*, whose pods are more or less straight.

Tests have shown that the greatest amount of poison is found in the seeds although pods and foliage are also toxic. The poisonous element is fluorocetate. Sheep and cattle have been known to die in less than 5 minutes after eating the seeds and more deaths occur during the dry season or in periods of drought.

Poison riceflower is its name

One small flowering shrub with red, succulent but poisonous fruits is the poison riceflower, *Pimelea pauciflora*. It's also called scrub kurrajong and scanty riceflower, and is a bright green shrub reaching about 1.2 metres in height with narrow, pointed leaves about 2 centimetres long.

The inconspicuous flowers are greenish-yellow, male and female ones being carried on separate bushes. It grows in all eastern states including Tasmania. While there have been reports of stock losses assumed to be caused by eating the fruits, children who have swallowed the attractive red berries have suffered abdominal pains but later recovered.

Other riceflowers suspected of toxicity include the yellow riceflower, *P. flava*, whose clusters of bright yellow flowers are backed by four rounded, yellow-green bracts.

Toxic red fruit of the tie-bush

The tie-bush, *Wikstroemia indica*, like the poison riceflower, is a slightly smaller, much-branched shrub with 5 centimetre long leaves in pairs. The small greenish-yellow flowers are followed by showy red fruit about 6mm long, each holding a single seed within its fleshy outer coat.

The tie-bush is common in moderate rainfall areas of eastern Australia from the central coast of New South Wales north through Queensland to the Northern Territory. Exactly what poison is contained in the plant is uncertain but while the foliage is less toxic there have been reports of children dying after eating the fruits.

Nauseating white cedar

One of Australia's few deciduous trees the white cedar, *Melia azedarach* var. *australasica*, bears dull yellow, oval fruits about 1.5 centimetres long containing some so far unrecognised toxin which is reported to have poisoned pigs, sheep, cattle and children, causing nausea, gastric disturbance, severe thirst, sweating, drowsiness and convulsions.

ANT R & D Keller

ANT I. R. McCann

ANT Ivan Polunin

Often planted in parks, the seeds of the Moreton Bay chestnut or black bean tree (above) can cause pain and dizziness if eaten, even in small quantities.

Although poisonous the common nardoo was often eaten by inland Aboriginals who collected the fruit, ground and mixed it into a paste.

The sap of the fish poison tree was used effectively by Aboriginals to stun fish and bring them to the surface.

Found in drier regions of New South Wales and Queensland, the flesh of berries from the strychnine tree (right) is harmless but the seeds are exceedingly poisonous.

Sometimes known as the Persian lilac, bead-tree or China berry, the white cedar is a broad-headed shade tree native to New South Wales south coast and north Queensland but widely planted because of its ability to thrive in dry climates. The large, loose clusters of starry flowers are orchid pink and faintly perfumed. The fruits appearing in autumn are green at first but ripen to dull yellow.

Chestnut tree toxin

Often planted as a shade tree in parks or around playing fields, the natural habitat of the Moreton Bay Chestnut or black bean, *Castanospermum australe*, is from northern New South Wales to Cooktown in Queensland, in rainforests or near waterways. It is a large, 30 metres tall, evergreen tree with a spreading head, glossy dark green foliage and brilliant orange pea flowers half hidden among the leaves.

The big pods, sometimes 25 centimetres long, contain 2–6 large, chestnut-like seeds, about 4 centimetres long. A thin, brown outer husk covers the pale creamy flesh of the cotyledons, seed leaves. While the actual poison in the seeds is unknown, the results if they are eaten raw is very unpleasant. Cases of vomiting, diarrhoea, abdominal pains and dizziness have all been recorded following the eating of small quantities.

Imported poisonous plants

Many cultivated plants imported from outside Australia also bear fruits whose contents are harmful to humans, especially children. These include several species of angel's trumpets, *Brugmansia*, and thornapple whose seeds, like those of the native species, are particularly toxic to man, causing thirst, delirium, and hallucinations, followed in some cases by coma and death.

The laburnum or golden chain tree, *Laburnum anagyroides*, whose long strings of yellow pea flowers are followed by seeds containing the toxic alkaloid cytisine which can be lethal. The castor oil plant, *Ricinus communis* is a big shrub with large, palmately lobed leaves and hard oval seeds to 1 centimetre long enclosed in spiky capsules; these are particularly poisonous — fewer than four seeds can kill a child — so they should be cut from the bushes before they mature.

Fatal fern foliage

While it is well known that certain seeds are poisonous, it is not always appreciated that ferns too can contain harmful substances in their foliage. One of the most widespread of all the ferns, bracken, *Pteridium*, includes several species which if eaten over long periods by livestock can cause various forms of poisoning such as bracken staggers in horses and bracken rhizome poisoning in pigs. It is even believed in Japan that the milk of bracken fed cows and tinned bracken shoots may be connected with stomach cancer in humans.

Other ferns with poisonous properties include the mulga or rock fern, *Cheilanthes sieberi*, often confused with *C. tenufolia*. This is a small, tufted fern with scaly rhizomes and dark-green, deeply divided upright, triangular fronds up to 40 centimetres long but only 3–4 centimetres wide. It is common in eastern Australia and is known to cause death when eaten in large amounts by stock (usually when no other feed is available).

The fruiting bodies of the common nardoo, *Marsilea drummondii*, were part of the diet of aborigines of the arid inland. The plants are usually found in areas where temporary flooding occurs, the four, wedge-shaped sections of the long stalked leaves floating on the surface of the water. The fruiting bodies growing on long stalks from the rhizomes were collected by the aborigines, ground and mixed into a paste. These plants are often eaten by stock without harmful results but when they have formed the sole available plant, as in times of excessive rainfall, they have caused stock losses. ●

ANT Keith Williams

PLANTS OF PREY

Extraordinary carnivorous flora

A.N.T. Kathie Atkinson

Many fantastic and gruesome stories have been told of large silent plants whose leaves suddenly spring to life and enfold even humans within their grasp. No trace of the victim remains except perhaps for a pair of boots or some buttons, later discarded by the plant when it unfolds itself to wait for the next unwary passerby. Such stories of plants that eat men may be untrue but the existence of carnivorous plants is fact. The extraordinary mechanisms by which they trap their prey led Charles Darwin to say 'hardly any more remarkable fact than this has been observed in the vegetable kingdom'.

Most of those plants found in Australia, however, live on a mild diet of insects and some such as the sundew or pitcher make excellent substitutes for chemical flysprays when cultivated in the home. Only the bladderwort in this country has been known to extend its appetite beyond insects to tadpoles and small fish.

The flypaper traps

There are several different ways in which these plants trap their prey. The sundew and the rainbow plant use what is known as the flypaper

The Venus fly trap, *Dionaea muscipula* effectively impales an unsuspecting fly in its natural cage.

If an insect touches only one tentacle on the leaf of the pimpernel sundew (left), it is trapped within seconds.

The black-eyed sundew (right), has beautiful, satiny flowers which early settlers pressed and used for ink.

Each tentacle of the sundew (left) transmits a stimulus to the others. In response, they bend towards the centre and secure the victim.

Some Australian species of *Drosera* such as the colourful pink rainbow are grown from seed and used as attractive garden displays.

There are 60 to 70 different species of *Drosera* including the *D. erythrorhiza*. All bear fine hairs covered by sticky drops of fluid which glisten to attract insects.

trap. The upper surface of their leaves is covered with fine hairy tentacles tipped with sticky glands to which the prey becomes glued.

Of the 90 kinds of sundew in the world 56 are found in Australia. These plants have beautiful, scarlet, satiny flowers which the early settlers pressed and used for ink. Sundews come under the botanic name Drosera meaning 'dewy'. Whereas the rainbow plant is a passive trap, it does not move, the sundew is an active trap, the tentacles wrap themselves around the prey. If an insect touches even one tentacle on the leaf, it is entangled within seconds. Each tentacle transmits a stimulus to the others and in response they will bend towards the centre to help secure the victim. After some hours all are curved tightly inwards in a symmetrical fashion.

So sensitive are these tentacles to touch that when Darwin, in his experiments, introduced a minute fragment of hair he evoked a response. Each tentacle secretes in the gland at its tip a digestive juice. Over a period of days the soluble matter of the prey is reduced to a fluid that is absorbed by the plant. The tentacles then assume their original position, fanned out and glue-tipped, ready for the next meal.

However there is one insect, the assassin bug, which is immune. This insect lives only on sundews and is coloured green with red dots in perfect imitation of sundew leaves. It hides on the underside of the stem until hungry and then it runs up and down the stem until it finds a trapped insect. It then sinks its long proboscis into the body of the insect and sucks. On the rainbow plant too, there is one small wingless insect, the capsid or leaf bug which moves freely over the sticky glands without becoming entangled. The secret of its immunity is unknown.

The pitfall traps

The pitcher plants are known as the pitfall traps in that the victim falls to its death, into a juice inside the pitcher leaves. The Western Australian pitcher plant grows in peaty swamps of the south coast. It is a low plant with thick branching roots bearing numerous clusters of pitches. It has two kinds of leaves, the conventional oval, shining green ones and the pitcher leaves which are sometimes mistaken for flowers. The actual flowers are inconspicuous, whitish-green and very small, whereas the pitcher leaf, when the plant grows in the sun, is brilliant shades of red and purple.

The leaf grows to five centimetres in length and looks like a lidded scoop-shaped jug. When the leaf is mature the lid rises a little and acts as an awning over the pitcher which accumulates fluid. This fluid eventually contains insect remains, hard horny parts, ants' heads and wing covers of beetles but there is no smell of decay.

Why do insects go into the trap? Crawling insects such as ants feed on the outer surface of the leaf and then crawl down the side of the pitcher to feed on the nectar in the glands halfway down, and then fall in. Flying insects have been observed to hover repeatedly at the mouth of the pitcher before finally giving in to temptation and entering their doom.

Tropical pitcher, a devil's jug

The Australian species of tropical pitcher plant, *Nepenthes mirabilis*, also known as monkey rice pot and devil's jug, is used in many ways. The pitchers are collected as children's playthings, the roots boiled and eaten for dysentery or to ease sore mouths and swelling and on one island rice is cooked in the pitcher and said to be delicious eaten with bananas and jungle fruit.

These plants usually need a tropical climate but two plants have been reported growing on a trellis in Parramatta, Sydney. Queensland pitchers grow up to 18 centimetres but in the East Indies some spectacular species grow to twice that length and have been credited with trapping birds and small mammals.

Live creatures make their home within the pitcher. There are certain species of spiders which live nowhere else and swimming among the insect remains are the larvae of certain flies and mosquitoes.

The suction traps

The bladderworts or Utricularia are known as suction traps. These plants grow on mossy banks, on the edges of swamps or float in the water. They have no roots but fibrous root-like growths, and brightly coloured two-lipped flowers in purples, golds and blues. The bladdder traps, an unusual leaf form, are smaller than a grain of wheat. They are hollow with the

The pitcher plant has a pitcher-like vessel that traps insects which the plant then digests, obtaining nutrients it's unable to get from the soil.

The tropical pitcher plant, *Nepenthes mirabilis* thrives in swampy humid conditions and has pitchers which grow to a length of 20 centimetres.

Commonly known as fairies' aprons, these bladderworts or *Utricularia* have a trap which secretes water. At the faintest touch, the victim is sucked in with the manufactured water.

The colourful Albany pitcher plant or Albany flycatcher is found in swampy areas around the coastal district of Albany, Western Australia.

122

A crane fly hopelessly enmeshed in the sticky tentacles of a sundew plant (above).

The assassin bug is immune to the sundew trap.

These pitcher plants of the genus *Sarracenia* have long pitchers protected by kidney-shaped lids. They require a cool, moist atmosphere with humidity and are sometimes grown in pots indoors.

entrance guarded by a hanging door which is attached overhead and at the sides.

The trap excretes water from inside the bladder through the walls. On the door are bristles and glands which throw off sugar and mucilage to attract insects. At the faintest touch of a bristle the door buckles inwards, water rushes in and the victim goes in too. Then the water is gradually expelled and the bladder resets itself. The spring opens and closes the door in less than ⅓₃ second.

One species of suction traps, *U. area* has been responsible for the elimination or at least the destruction of the tadpoles of the toad, *Bufo marinus.* Upon passing the suction trap the tadpoles were sucked in either by the head or tail and died in their watery grave. Many small fish have been eliminated in the same way.

The spring traps

The Venus fly trap and the waterwheel plant both have incredibly ingenious and efficient traps known as spring traps. The Venus fly trap, *Dionaea muscipula*, is a terrestrial plant originating in the coastal areas of Carolina in the United States, where it grows in damp sandy soil. Recently its numbers have been found to be rapidly diminishing and it is on the verge of extinction despite its magnificent trap.

This trap consists of twin lobes held ajar. When the prey enters the compass of these lobes it trips a trigger mechanism and the lobes snap shut like a pair of jaws, imprisoning the victim. The lobes secrete a sweet nectar which attracts prey. The trigger mechanism consists of bristle-like hairs which when touched spring the trap.

The waterwheel, *Aldrovanda vesiculosa*, is a rootless plant resembling a bottlebrush, found in freshwater swamps and lagoons of northern Australia. The leaves are arranged in whorls along the stem like wheels on an axis. The leaf stalk is long and wedge-shaped and bears at the end a round leaf-blade which has 40 long sensitive hairs in the middle. When an insect touches one of these, the sides of the leaf quickly fold into the centre to entrap the insect. Interlocking spines on the margins of the leaf prevent escape and water is expelled quickly through each end as the victim is carried down into the centre of the leaf where a cavity is formed. It takes ⅕₀th second for the leaf to shut on a victim. The sides squeeze together, pressing the prey closer into the cavity where the digestive and absorptive glands are located.

The Venus fly trap, the pitcher and some species of sundew can be bought at certain specialised nurseries and are very satisfying to grow. They are, on the whole, not difficult to cultivate and almost all of them are very beautiful and richly coloured. They usually require high humidity and do not like a fierce sun. ●

THE FASCINATION OF FUNGI

Beautiful to look at but dangerous to touch, the fly agaric.

Emperor Claudius died of mushroom poisoning and so did Pope Clement VII in 1534; history will never record with any certainty how many kings, rulers, potentates, tyrants and courtiers had met an early and convulsive death by fungi poisoning either through accident or arranged.

Of course, thousands of others must have also met the same fate, people of ordinary or lowly ranks whose only mistake was not being able to tell the difference between edible and deadly fungi.

The world knows of about 100 000 different species of these organisms of which mushrooms and toadstools are only a small part.

Fungi are flowerless and leafless; they have no chlorophyll and they reproduce by means of spores. Many types of fungi are microscopically small while others grow to visible size; these include the common mushrooms. Those which cannot be seen by the naked eye include bacteria, moulds, mildews, yeast, smuts and rusts; invisibly small — except for the result of their work.

Nourishment from the dead

Ordinary plants manufacture their own food supply — but fungi cannot and most derive their nourishment from dead organic matter. Others rely completely or partly on living plants and animals; these we know as parasites. Some parasitic fungi grow only on the surface of their host while others enter through the outer layer of the plant or animal skin, even natural openings.

Most plant diseases are caused by fungi. The basic fungal growth is a network of fine, thread-like tubes called hyphae; a mass of these is called a mycelium which grows outwards from a central point in all directions, producing the circular appearance of most fungal growth.

The devastating effects of fungi on plants can be seen as symptoms such as scabs, rots, cankers, galls or distortions like curling leaves.

Fungi are divided into groups according to their reproductive structures.

They include the Myxomycetes or slime moulds which get their food only from dead organic material; the Zygomycetes, such as bread moulds attacking fruit already picked; the Oomycetes, like the downy mildews attacking living plants; the Ascomycetes which produce the powdery mildews, brown rot of stone fruit; and the Basidiomycetes, a group which embraces mushrooms and toadstools as well as rusts and smuts.

Life-saving drugs

Fungi can be useful to man. They are used to manufacture cheese and yoghurt and also in antibiotics; yeasts produce vitamin B and some types of fungi assist plants to obtain nutrients from the soil. In the last few decades life-saving drugs like penicillin and streptomycin have been fungi derivations.

At the same time, some species cause severe illnesses in humans. Serious bacterial diseases traced to fungi include tuberculosis, meningitis, leprosy and diphtheria.

The must dangerous, indeed, deadly fungi are the poisonous mushrooms. Leading the parade of villains is the death cup or death cap (*Amanita phalloides*), also known as the angel of death. The cap of this mushroom grows to 12 centimetres

A bright red Agaric fungi is definitely not one of the edible variety, although the common edible mushroom is a member of the same group. Research into fungi is still limited but this species is apparently found in wet open forests in Victoria. Recommend inedible.

Mycena subgalericulata is an Agaric fungi which is widespread in rainforests in NSW, Victoria and SA. This fungi has no smell and no taste but is regarded as inedible.

The underside of a *Laccaria laccata* fungus (Agaric) showing the gills which fan out from the stalk. Spores are produced by the gills. Some reports say that edible mushrooms have pink gills but this is not a hard fast rule. Authorities recommend inedible.

Brick-red tuft fungus, *Naematoloma sublateritium*, is a member of the Agaric group and is found in Tasmania, SA and Victoria and grows on the wood at the base of trees. These mushrooms are used in cooking by Italians in Europe and America, but authorities recommend local varieties inedible.

Aleuria rhenana (left) is a cup fungi which grows on the ground and unlike the familiar cap fungi has no stalk or strip. Spores are formed inside the the cup or bowl. These fungi are found in Victoria in wet forests. Recommend inedible.

The pencil fungi or coral fungi (left) is a member of the Clavaria group. This fungi is found in Tasmania, Victoria, NSW and SA. Recommend inedible.

The basket fungi or maiden's veil fungi (right) is found in rainforests in Queensland and NSW and is a stinkhorn fungi. The odour of this attractive mushroom is likened to the smell of rotting meat.

These fungi (left) start out as small blob then burst open. A secretion which attracts flies also contains the spores and when the flies leave the spores are stuck to their bodies.

Yellow brain fungi (right) is a jelly fungi. The fruit bodies look like jelly and when they have dried out they shrivel until rain falls and they can take in the water and resume normal shape.

Flame fungi (left) is a member of the Clavaria group and is found in areas of high rainfall in Victoria, NSW, SA and Tasmania. This fungi is classed as club fungi as they have no cap and no strip.

Luminous fungi, *Mycena chlorophianus* (right) is found in tropical rainforests in Queensland. This photo was taken at night with an exposure of 20 minutes.

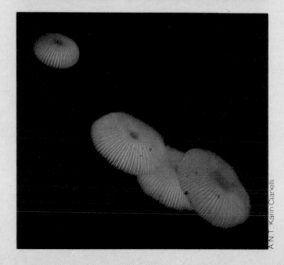

A bracket fungi, *Trametes cinnabarina* (left) grows out of tree trunks and in some cases their presence can mean death for the tree. It has been reported that these bracket fungi can change the colour of the tree's timber. Found in all States except the Northern Territory. Recommend inedible.

Cartinarius archeri (left) is found in SA, Victoria, Tasmania and NSW. The spores of this species are contained in the cottonwool-like cloud over the mushroom. Recommend inedible.

Ken Griffiths

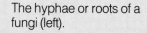

The hyphae or roots of a fungi (left).

The petalled puff ball or earth star fungi (right) start out as a smooth ball then the outer layer of skin splits and folds down to form the star shape. The spores are contained within the centre bulb and released in puffs when needed.

ANT

poisonous, its gills are white. They were believed to be unknown in Australia until 1967 when they were located around Canberra; it is assumed that the species had been introduced in seed form accidentally.

Some 90 percent of mushroom fatalities around the world are caused by this species or its close relatives. Claudius of the Roman Empire and Pope Clement VII were among its best known victims.

The death cap

Frighteningly, the death cap claims its victim hours before he even suspects anything. The first symptoms — nausea, fever, convulsion — are not produced until 6 to 15 hours after the mushroom had been eaten. By this time the poison had been absorbed in the blood stream and circulated throughout the body; even the most thorough stomach pump is now ineffective.

The poison damages the liver and the kidneys, causing immense pain. After perhaps two days or so, the nervous system becomes paralysed, the patient lapses into a coma — and may die a week or 10 days later.

There are several other poisonous species of mushrooms though not many of those found in Australia can cause fatal accidents. Europe and the Americas, on the other hand, have dozens of mildly or severely toxic mushrooms.

The best prevention is a knowledge of poisonous mushrooms; those which are sold to the public should be safe. The danger lurks in forests where bushwalkers or picnickers find some lovely-looking mushrooms and eat them without any precaution. Boiling, cooking or even baking them doesn't make them any less deadly; the toxic chemicals hiding in the mushrooms will survive any treatment and set about taking their ultimate revenge: they destroy those who want to destroy them. ●

Bay Picture Library

INDEX